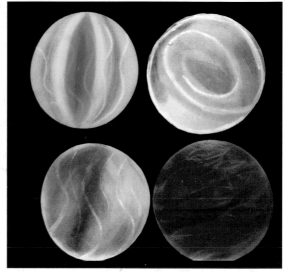

Drawing Marbles from Observation

Equipment Needed
Grey sugar paper cut into squares and circles. Chalks or chalk pastels, paper towels and hair spray as a fixative. A collection of marbles of different sizes.

Talk About

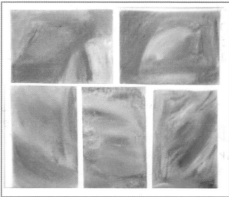

- The links between toys that are played with today and similar toys played with by parents and grandparents e.g. marbles, to develop the concept of past and present.
- What these toys are and how they are played with.
- The shape of the marbles, the different sizes of the marbles and the patterns on them.
- The games they play with marbles and the games their parents or grandparents played with them.
- What the marbles are made of.
- Their favourite marble in the collection and why they like it.
- The drawing media they are going to use for their work.

Doing
- Choose a piece of square sugar paper and some chalk pastels.
- Experiment by adding patches of colour to the paper, by using the pastels in a variety of ways e.g. using the tip of the pastels, using the pastels on their side, pressing on them firmly and pressing on them gently.
- Explore smudging and blending some of the patches of colour together to make new colours, using either a finger or a paper towel.
- Choose a marble and look at it carefully. Draw the swirls and shapes you see on the marble with your finger on a circular piece of paper before doing the same using the pastels.
- Work from the top of the circle downwards to avoid smudging your work.
- Press down firmly for a rich covering of colour.
- Smudge some of the colours together and leave others as they are.
- Finally draw in any lines and swirls observed using the tip of the pastels.

Display
Before the work is put on display it will need a light covering of hair spray to fix the colours. Do this in a well ventilated area when the children are not around. Display the work unmounted in a large circle on the board. In the centre of the circle arrange mounted photographs of the children working on their drawings and playing with the marbles. Include their written comments alongside the photographs.

Printing Teddy Bears

Equipment Needed

Coloured sugar paper (A3 size), pieces of sponge. Red, yellow, blue, black and white ready mix paint, pieces of card to use as mixing palettes, paintbrushes and a collection of teddy bears.

Talk About

- The appearance of the different teddy bears in the collection to develop the concept of old and new. Sort the bears into two groups and describe their differences e.g. those that look well worn and those that are pristine or recently acquired.
- The bear they brought for the collection or the one they like best - and why.
- The colours, shapes, sizes of the different bears.
- The texture of the bears, how they look and feel e.g. soft, furry, tickly etc.
- How to print with a piece of sponge, by dipping it in paint and then pressing it on and off **not** smearing and spreading it on the paper.
- Mixing different colours of paint together on a card palette with a paint brush to make new colours.
- The size that the work needs to be on the background paper.

Doing

- Choose a teddy bear from the collection, look at it carefully and feel its outline shape.
- Get a piece of coloured sugar paper, arrange it portrait way up and using only a finger, draw the shape of the teddy bear you have been looking at. Make sure your drawing fills most of the paper.
- Put some paint on a card palette and using a brush mix the colours together until they

have made the colour that closely matches your bear. Remember to make plenty of this colour before you start!

- Get a piece of sponge, dip it in the paint and begin to print the shape of your bear. Start with the head and remember to leave plenty of room to add on the body and legs. Finally add the arms and the ears. Your completed sponge-printed bear shape should have a furry texture similar to your actual teddy bear.
- Dip your finger in paint to print the nose and the eyes and use the paintbrush to draw in the mouth and any other details.

Display

Display the prints in a row or a block behind an arrangement of the actual bears that the children have used for their work. Use printed or cut out versions of the 'texture' words collected with the children as a border.

Contents

Step by Step Art Books are available from all good Educational Bookshops and by mail order from:

Topical Resources, P.O. Box 329, Broughton, Preston, Lancashire. PR3 5LT

Topical Resources publishes a range of Educational Materials for use in Primary Schools and Pre-School Nurseries and Playgroups.

For the latest catalogue
Tel 01772 863158 / Fax 01772 866153
e.mail: sales@topical-resources.co.uk
Visit our Website at: www.topical-resources.co.uk

Copyright © 2004 Dianne Williams

Printed in Great Britain for 'Topical Resources', Publishers of Educational Materials, P.O. Box 329, Broughton, Preston, Lancashire PR3 5LT by T.Snape & Company Limited, Boltons Court, Preston Lancashire.

Typeset by Paul Sealey Illustration & Design, 3 Wentworth Drive, Thornton, Lancashire.

First Published September 2004.

ISBN 1 872977 87 1

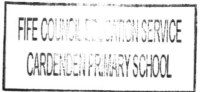

Introduction

History has always had strong links with Art and Design. It is from the work of artists, craft workers and designers from the past that many clues about how people lived, dressed, travelled, ate, entertained etc. in previous times can be gathered. Looking at pictures and artefacts from the past is a vital part of any history topic and in turn these provide a rich stimulus for art and design activities. This book aims to provide ideas for a number of simple, easy to follow, skill based art activities linked to a range of different history topics relevant to the National Curriculum for History at Key Stage One and Key Stage Two.

The practical activities are designed to introduce and encourage children to explore many different techniques using a range of both two and three dimensional materials. These include drawing, painting, printing, collage, textiles and 3D as well as ICT activities where appropriate.

There are several separate activities for each of the topics. Each activity has its links with history explained in a 'talk about' section, a list of the materials needed, instructions on how to undertake the work plus suggestions as to how the finished work could be displayed. The activities, the skills involved and the materials used, cover much of the content of the National Curriculum for Art and Design at Key Stage One and Key Stage Two.

Each activity is illustrated for guidance. All the activities have been used by teachers in school and their response has been enthusiastic. History displays resulting from the activities, they suggest, have had considerable impact on the topic being studied and have helped support and reinforce the children's learning. Visually, the displays of finished work have greatly enriched the classroom environment. I hope these activities when undertaken, will do the same for you and your classes.

Dianne Williams

Schools which have provided work for this book include:
- Moss Side Community Primary School
- Balshaw Lane Community Primary School
- Brabbins Endowed Primary School
- Seven Stars Primary School
- Revoe Community Primary School
- Parbold R.C. Primary School
- Deepdale Infant School
- Ashton Community Primary School
- Bowerham Community Primary School
- St. Theresas R.C. Primary, Up Holland
- Slyne with Hest Primary School
- Gillibrand Community Primary School
- Skerton Community Primary School
- Parbold Primary School

Many other Lancashire schools have also offered inspiration for this work.

Toys

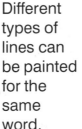

Painting Marks to Represent the Different Ways in Which Toys Move

Equipment Needed

Large pieces of white paper - sugar paper or paper of 80-120 gsm in weight (newsprint will tend to be flimsy), paintbrushes, ready-mix paint in assorted colours, plastic pots for the paint.

Talk About

*   The different ways one toy e.g. a ball can be made to move - bouncing, rolling, throwing etc, and the ways that other toys in the setting can be made to move e.g. spinning, rocking, pushing, pulling, wound up etc.
*   How many modern toys now need batteries or switches to make them work whereas toys in the past didn't. Realising that toys have changed.
*   The sort of toys that need batteries and the sort that don't.
*   Drawing different lines with a paintbrush.
*   Working in turn collaboratively on any part of a large piece of paper.
*   Making sure that the lines don't cross over.
*   Making lines that are similar next to other lines but in a different colour.

Doing

*   In turn each child chooses a paintbrush and one pot of paint and goes to a place on the large paper.
*   They name a toy movement already described e.g. spinning and paint a line on the paper to represent the movement. The line can be long or short and can go in any direction on the paper.
*   The teacher may need to help with the words if the children find this difficult.

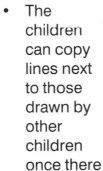

Different types of lines can be painted for the same word.

*   The children can copy lines next to those drawn by other children once there are plenty of lines covering the paper.
*   Encourage the children to use a different colour each time they paint but to return each brush to its own pot colour so that the colours don't become dirty.
*   Encourage the children to explore mixing colours in some of the pots for a rich variety of colour. Again remind them to leave the brushes in each new mixture so that they can be used by others. Work until the entire paper is covered and filled.

Display

As this is a large scale piece of work it would be difficult to mount. It would be advisable to attach it to the wall and then add a plain strip of paper around the edge as a border. The 'movement words' identified by the children could be printed out using the computer and added to the border.

Cutting and Colour Matching Jigsaws

Equipment Needed
White paper - A4 size and slightly larger, coloured wax crayons, scissors, glue, an assortment of trimmed coloured magazine pictures and old greetings cards plus a range of jigsaws from the very simple to the more complex.

Talk About
- The different types of jigsaws in the collection and what they are made of.
- Discuss who might play with each type e.g. which jigsaws might be suitable for a very young child, which ones could they themselves manage and which ones are more difficult and are suitable for adults.
- Sorting the jigsaws into groups as above to develop an awareness of chronological order.
- Comparing the simple shapes that make up the easy jigsaws and the more complicated shapes found in the more difficult ones.
- Talk about the jigsaws in their setting - those that are easy and those that are more difficult.
- Cutting a picture into simple shapes to make a jigsaw.
- Finding the wax crayon colours that match the colours in a cut up picture.

Doing
- Choose a magazine picture or a greetings card from the collection.
- Cut it into several large pieces of any shape - aim for more than three pieces but less than ten!
- Get a piece of white paper and arrange the pieces on it leaving large gaps between each one. Glue the pieces down carefully.
- Look carefully at one of the pieces of your stuck down jigsaw and find the wax crayon colours that match the colours you see on it.
- Use these colours to make a border or several rings round this piece using each of the colours. Press down firmly for a rich covering of colour.
- Continue working in the same way until you have surrounded each piece of your jigsaw.

Display
Trim and mount each colour matched jigsaw individually. Print or cut out the words 'Just Jigsaws' and arrange them in the middle of the board. Cut out some large black jigsaw pieces to go next to them. Arrange the mounted children's work in rows around this central title. Keep the spaces between them to a minimum to give the display maximum impact.

Build a Giant Lego Model

Equipment Needed
Reclaimed materials i.e. cardboard boxes, masking tape, glue, scissors, white tissue paper or newsprint, ready-mix paint, large paintbrushes and paint pots. A collection of different bricks e.g. soft fabric ones, wooden ones and large and small plastic ones etc.

Talk About
- What is similar and what is different about the building bricks in the collection.
- Who might the different types of bricks be appropriate for i.e. which age group might play with them and why.
- Which bricks are the most modern and which type were probably played with by grandparents and why (developing an awareness of the different materials used to make toys now and in the past).
- The way the different bricks can be made to fit together, which ones they most like to play with and what they like to make with them.
- Making a figure using Lego bricks. The different body parts their figure will have and the need to use different sizes of bricks for the different parts.

Doing
- Look at the different Lego figures the children have made and together choose one to build on a large scale out of reclaimed materials. The children will need to take turns in small groups working with an adult to build the large scale model.
- From a collection of boxes of different sizes select those that match the parts of the figure to be made and arrange them to make its shape as though it is lying down on the floor. Make sure that large strong boxes are used for the feet to give the model stability when it is upright.

- When all the boxes have been assembled fasten them together vertically with masking tape, so that the robot is built in an upright position.
- If it is built a section at a time, each section could have a covering of paper and glue to make it more stable and robust.
- The robot when complete will need painting in colours that match those of the original body.
- Large brushes and plenty of paint will be needed. Encourage the children to paint the model in sections and allow each section to dry before painting the next.

Display
For health and safety reasons, this large scale model is better displayed in a non-traffic area e.g. in a corner against a wall. Display the other Lego figures on covered boxes around its feet. Back the board in a matching colour.

Key Stage 1
Toys

Painting and Collage Combined

Equipment Needed

White paper A4 size, toy catalogues and colour magazines, scissors, glue, glue spreaders, wax crayons (thick and thin), paint, paintbrushes and pieces of card as mixing palettes, white paper A3 size plus a collection of old Christmas cards that feature toy shop windows from the past with adults and children looking in them .

Talk About

- The toys on display in the shop windows on the cards - those that are similar to toys the children still play with now and those that are different.
- The types of shops where children nowadays see toys on display.
- The clothes that the children and adults are wearing on the cards - are they similar or different from those worn today? Do the settings on the cards show the present or the past? What are the clues?
- Talk about the types of toys that might be in the window and the sorts of clothes the shoppers might be wearing if the cards were modern ones.
- Cutting shapes out of magazines and sticking them on to a background - how much glue to use and where to put it.

Doing

- Choose a Christmas card showing shoppers looking in a toy shop window. Look carefully at the shape of the window, the size and arrangement of the toys in it and the size of the shoppers outside it.
- Get a toy catalogue and cut out pictures of toys to fit on a piece of A4 paper as part of the toy shop window.
- Arrange the cut out toys on your paper in groups or rows. When you are pleased with your arrangement get some glue and a glue spreader and stick it down. Draw shelves in wax crayon under the toys for them to rest on.
- Finally draw the shape of a person in modern dress with a paintbrush on a piece of A3 paper. Fill in the shape. Add details e.g. patterns on clothes and features. Cut the figure out when it is dry.

Display

Mount the Christmas cards the children have used as a stimulus and display them in a block at one side of the board. Add the word 'Then' in large letters above this group. Combine the A4 collages of toys together in a block to make a shop window. Arrange strips of black paper around and across the block to complete the window. Arrange the cut out painted figures in front of and beside this window as in the original cards. Add the word 'Now' in large letters above this part of the board.

Key Stage 1
Houses and Homes

Around and About - Mixed Media Work From Memory and Observation

Equipment Needed

Paint, paintbrushes, pieces of card as palettes, wax crayons, oil pastels, white paper A3 size or larger, collage materials, scissors, glue, glue spreaders and photographs of different houses in the locality taken on a class walk if possible.

Talk About

- The different types of house that people live in today.
- The different types of houses in the area near school and in the photographs of the locality. Where these houses can be seen and what each type is called e.g. bungalow, flat etc
- The houses that are similar to each other and those that are different.
- Those that the children think are old and those that are new - and why.
- The type of house they live in and whether it is a new house or one that was lived in before they moved there.
- Mixing paint on a card palette. Painting large shapes first then adding details e.g. bricks by drawing or working with collage materials on top of the paint once it is dry.
- Cutting the collage materials into different shapes and gluing them on. How much glue to use and where to put it.
- Either working from a photograph or from memory how to paint a picture of their own house or a house in the locality.

Doing

- Take a piece of paper and with only a finger draw the shape of a house to make sure it is big enough to fill most of the page.
- Get some paint and a paintbrush and draw and fill in the main shapes of your house on the paper.
- Decide on the details you now need to add to your house e.g. doors, windows, drainpipes etc. Either draw these on top of your painting using a crayon or oil pastel or add them using collage materials.
- Add the pavement and or garden and sky to complete your picture and fill the paper.

Display

Arrange the photographs of the houses in the locality in the centre of the board. Mount and arrange the children's paintings as a border around them.

Finally, around the outer edge of the display, use cut out letters or computer printed labels that give the names of the different types of houses discussed and found in the locality.

Using Door Shapes for Pattern Work

Equipment Needed

White paper A3 size or larger. If the children are going out sketching smaller pieces A4 size and drawing boards or thick card to rest on plus clips to attach the paper to the boards. Drawing pencils, paint, paintbrushes and pieces of card as palettes. Pictures of different types of doors - DIY shops are a good source for these as well as pictures of doors in the locality.

Talk About

- The type of front door that is on their own house. The different types of doors in the DIY catalogues. Doors that are similar to these that are on houses in the area (following a walk in the locality). Those they like best and why. Encourage the children to collect information about the houses using the outside of them for clues.
- Discuss houses in the locality that are similar in design but have different types of front doors. Why might they have been changed? Which are new and which are old - and why? What are the doors made of? What shapes go next to and around the door?
- Drawing several different types of doors in the locality and the shapes around them - **not** complete houses. Use photographs if it is more appropriate.
- Choosing and drawing the outline of one door shape from the collection on a larger scale in paint. Outlining the main shapes that are on the door. Adding the shapes that go next to the door. Decorating and filling these shapes with lines and smaller shapes to create a pattern inside and around the door.

Doing

- Choose one doorway to work on from the sketches you have made. Draw its outline first with a finger on an A3 piece of paper - portrait way up - to get an idea of the size it will need to be before drawing it with a paintbrush.
- Outline the main shapes on the door e.g. the panels, letterbox, doorknob, windows etc. and the shapes next to the door. Go round and add to each of these shapes in turn using lines and small shapes to make different patterns.
- Use several different colours for the lines and shapes.
- Fill in some of the shapes to make these patterns colourful and interesting.

Display

Mount each of the door paintings individually and display them in rows across the board. Under each painting, mount and display the original pencil sketches from which the work was developed.

Houses and Homes

Printing Brick Style Patterns and Creating Patterns from Rubbings

Equipment Needed

Black paint, paper plates to put the paint on, plasticene, white paper A4 size or A5, strips of paper (12cm wide 30cm long), wax crayons, real bricks and pictures of brick and stonework patterns.

Talk About

*   The building materials from which the school is made and the building materials used to make the houses in the locality.
*   The names of the different types of building materials - bricks, stone, tiles, PVC, flags, thatch, wood, glass etc. and what they would be used for.
*   The materials used to build houses today and those that were used to build houses in the past. Discuss old buildings that they may have visited or seen in films or on television and what they were made of.
*   Looking for and drawing the patterns made by tiles and brick work in and around school. Touching the patterns and describing the texture of the materials and how the shapes fit together, repeat and overlap.
*   Taking a rubbing from a brick by placing paper on top of it and pressing down firmly with a wax crayon.
*   Using two colours of crayon alternately.
*   Folding a strip of paper in half several times to divide it into segments.
*   Printing with a piece of plasticene dipped in paint.

Doing

*   Get a strip of paper and fold it in half several times. Open the strip out. It should now be divided up into segments,
*   Choose two colours of wax crayons and a brick. Put the first segment of the strip on to the brick and take a rubbing with one of the

crayons. Then move the next segment of the paper on to the brick and do the same but use the second colour. Move the paper along again and take another rubbing using your first colour again. Continue working this way until you reach the end of the strip.

*   Get a piece of plasticene and squeeze it into a brick/stone shape.
*   Dip it into black paint and on a piece of white paper, print a pattern of stone/brick shapes in rows next to and above and below each other. Turn the plasticene block on its side to print smaller shapes to fill the gaps as in a stone wall.

Display

Arrange the mounted work in groups with the accompanying pictures of brick, stone and tile patterns found in the locality.

Houses and Homes

Whose House?
Drawing from Imagination

Equipment Needed
White paper A4 size, drawing pencils and wax crayons. Stories and rhymes that feature different styles of houses e.g. Sleeping Beauty, The Three Little Pigs, Snow White, Rapunzel etc. Photographs of castles, cottages, forts etc. Pictures from colour magazines of cottages, castles etc.

Talk About
* The different styles of the houses in the stories and what they are called e.g. castles, palaces, cottages etc.
* The size of the different houses and what they were made of.
* Those that would be strong and last a long time and those that would soon fall to pieces.
* Houses in the photographs that are similar in style to the ones in the stories. Are they old or new? How can you tell?
* Who would live in these different styles of houses? What do these different styles of houses tell us about the people who live or lived in them?
* Which of these house styles are still being built today e.g. cottages and which styles were only built in the past? Why?
* Discuss new additions that are often made by the owners to a house e.g. porches, conservatories etc. Making children aware of changes that occur over time from the past to the present and into the future.

Doing
* Decide which type of house from a story or poem you are going to draw.
* Choose a piece of paper and with a drawing pencil sketch the outline of the house - and outside it the story character who lives in it.
* Have a photocopy made of this drawing before you add colour to it.

* Now colour in the original drawing carefully using wax crayons. Add extra details as you work e.g. stone work patterns, window panes etc.
* Now get the photocopied version of your original drawing and imagine you are the new owner of this house - how might you change it? What might you add to it to make it more up to date? A satellite dish, patio doors, an extension? etc.
* Draw these changes on your photocopied drawing.

Display
Mount both versions of each drawing and arrange them in rows, the originals above and the altered versions below. Cut out large letters that spell the word 'Changes' as the title of the display. Add a border around the edge of the display and on it add computer printed labels naming the characters and their houses that feature in the display.

Comparing and Drawing Old and New Household Objects that are Similar

Equipment Needed

Charcoal or black chalk pastels, chalk or white chalk pastels. Grey sugar paper or white paper A4 size. A collection of similar household objects of different ages and different styles e.g. a flat iron and an electric iron.

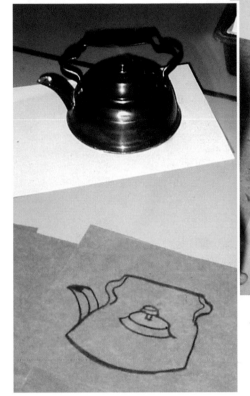

Talk About

- What the different objects are and what they are used for.
- What they are made of and how they feel to touch and hold.
- Which objects are old and which are new.
- How do we know, how can we tell?
- Sorting the objects into 'old' and 'new' sets.
- The shape of the objects and how the different parts fit together.
- The inside, outside and underneath of the objects.
- Making light and dark marks with the drawing media.
- Smudging light and dark marks together with a finger.

Doing

- Choose a household object from one of the sets and place it in front of you.
- Look carefully at the different parts of the object.
- Get a piece of paper, draw your object on it carefully with only your finger to get an idea of the size it will need to be.
- Now draw the outline of your object on your paper with a piece of white chalk or pastel.

- Colour in your object using both black and white pastel. Decide which parts need to be light (the outside edges, the top, shiny parts etc.) which bits need to be darker (grey) and which bits need to be very dark (under handles, the inside of an object etc.)
- Add lines and patterns to complete the details once the shape has been shaded in.
- Print a label on the computer to go with your object - it needs to say 'old' or 'new' depending on what you have drawn.

Display

Divide the display board into two using a strip of border roll. Add cut out letters that spell the word 'Old' to one half of the board and the word 'New' to the other half. Mount the individual drawings and display them on the part of the board they relate to. Display the sets of objects underneath the board.

Houses and Homes

Making a 3D Model of a Cooker or a Washing Machine

Equipment Needed

Cardboard boxes (washing powder and small cereal boxes are ideal), white paper to cover them with, glue, scissors, glue-spreaders, silver foil, clear cellophane, small pieces of card, paint, paintbrushes, small plastic lids (from bottles etc). Pictures of modern appliances and cookware.

Talk About

- The appliances used to wash clothes (automatic washers and driers) and to cook food (split level ovens, fan assisted ovens, microwaves etc.) in their own homes.
- How their grandparents washed clothes (twin tub washers) and cooked food (oil, electric or gas cookers) in the past and the sort of appliances they had to use.
- Pictures of even earlier times and the appliances that were then used for washing (dolly tubs) and cooking (coal and wood - burning stoves).
- Talk about how family life has changed and been made easier now machines help with the work and do it quickly.
- Look at and discuss the different types of appliances in pictures. Discuss the different features of the cookers and washers e.g. dials, doors that open, burners, hotplates, glass panels etc. and the parts of the appliance where they are found.

Doing

- Get a cardboard box to make into a cooker or washer. If it needs a door, cut out a door shape now (only cut 3 sides and leave it open but still attached to the original box). Cover the box with white paper.
- Use paint if you want to change the colour of

your appliance before using foil and plastic lids as knobs, dials etc. If the door needs to be transparent cut out the centre of it and replace it with cellophane.
- If you have made a washing machine cut out pictures of clothes or add pieces of fabric to go inside it.
- If you have made a cooker cut out pictures of saucepans, stick them on pieces of card, trim the card and then fasten them to the top of your cooker.

Display

Strips of paper can easily be attached to the back of each appliance so that they can be hung on the display board. Arrange them alongside drawings children have made of their kitchen at home or from a picture in a magazine. Alternatively the kitchen pictures could be done in collage using cut out cupboards/ appliances etc. Display pictures of old appliances under the board.

Famous Events & Famous People

Moon Landing

Equipment Needed

A computer graphics package that offers a star shape, a circle shape, a fill tool, and a spray tool (the programme Dazzle has been used here). Pictures of planets, night skies, space scenes and rockets in space.

Talk About

- When man first landed on the moon and who that man was - Neil Armstrong - and what his words were on landing.
- The country that he flew from and the name of his spacecraft - Apollo 11.
- What he might have seen from the windows of his spacecraft on the way to the moon.
- The tools to use on the computer for a space picture - the circle shape, the star shape, the fill tool and the spray tool - where they are found on the tool bar and how to get them.
- The colours found in the pictures of outer space. How to change to different colours on the computer by clicking on them using the left-hand mouse button.
- Experimenting with the different tools and colours before making a final piece of work.

Doing

- Use the left-hand mouse button all the time for this work. First click on the colour black, then the fill tool, then the screen, to fill with black.
- Click on a new colour and the circle shape. Return to the screen, click, hold down the button and drag out a circle shape. Let go of the button to keep the shape. Drag out more circles of different sizes on other parts of the screen.
- Click on a new colour, click on the fill tool, then click inside one of the circle shapes to fill it with colour. Repeat this process to fill the other circles.

- Click on the star shape and click on a colour. Return to the screen, click, hold down the button and drag out a star shape. Let go of the button to keep the shape. Draw further star shapes of different sizes on other parts of the screen. Fill these shapes in the same way as before.
- Finally click on the spray tool and click on a colour. Return to the screen, click and hold down the button to draw trails of spray over and around the stars. Use several different colours before printing out your work.

Display

Mount the work individually on red paper and use to create a border around a board on which there is written work about the moon landing.

Famous Events & Famous People

The Great Fire of London

Equipment Needed

Pieces of white paper and black paper, glue, scissors, black paint, pieces of card to put it on and small strips of card. Red and gold foil, red and yellow cellophane. Charcoal and white chalk. Pieces of red paper A4 size, pencils and pictures of the type of houses found in London at the time of the Fire of London.

Talk About

* Where the fire of London started and why it spread so quickly.
* The colours seen when there is a fire - warm colours, red, yellow and orange.
* The way smoke spirals upwards from a fire.
* The shapes and colours of the houses at this time, the style of windows they had and how they were very close together.
* What a gable end is and what it looks like.
* Cutting, tearing and crumpling foil and cellophane.
* The colour of smoke and how to make different shades of grey.
* Smudging patches of charcoal and chalk together.

Doing

* Get a piece of white paper and draw the gable end of a house on it. It needs to be about half the size of a piece of A4 paper portrait way up. Cut this shape out carefully.
* Tear some thin strips of black paper to add beams and to outline the roof and the door and windows.
* Use a thin strip of card dipped in black paint to print the criss-cross lines of the window panes.
* Tear some strips of foil and cellophane, and crumple them. Lay your house on the red paper and arrange these flames above and around it - and possibly coming through the door before sticking it all down on the background.
* Use chalk and charcoal smudged together to add smoke between and above the flames.

Display

Arrange the houses in a row each piece of red paper touching its neighbour across the top of a board. Cut some arches out of black paper to make a bridge across the board under the houses. Add some grey paper across the board under the bridge on which there could be a display of written work about the Great Fire of London.

George Stephenson and the Rocket

Equipment Needed
Pieces of white paper A3 size, circular lids, small thin strips of card, cotton bobbins, plasticene, black paint, orange paint and pieces of card to put it on. Pictures of Stephenson's Rocket railway engine.

Talk About
* Who George Stephenson was, when he lived and what he invented.
* The different types of transport that the children have seen, travelled on or travelled in.
* How people travelled before the invention of the railways.
* Where the nearest station is and where the trains go to.
* The different sizes of the wheels in the pictures of the Rocket and the patterns inside them.
* How to print with lids, strips of card, cotton bobbins and shapes made from plasticene by dipping them in paint before pressing them on to a piece of paper.
* Printing circular shapes on different parts of the paper, allowing some of them to touch or overlap.
* Printing small shapes inside larger ones.

Doing
* Get a piece of A3 paper, some lids of different sizes and some black paint and orange paint on a piece of card.
* Dip one of the lids into the black paint and then press it on to the paper in several different places to print a number of circles.
* Use other lids of different sizes in the same way - print some inside or overlapping some of the larger circles.
* Use a strip of card dipped in paint to print line patterns inside some circles.
* Use cotton bobbins and shapes made from plasticene in the same way.

* Use orange paint as well as black to make your patterns more interesting.
* Print patterns around the outside of some of the wheels as well.

Display
Mount each wheel pattern individually on orange paper and arrange them in rows with equal spaces between them as a broad border around the edge of a board covered with grey paper. Include pictures of the Rocket, writing about the engine and about George Stephenson and mount these on orange and black in the middle of the board.

Florence Nightingale

Equipment Needed

Pieces of black paper A4 size approx, pencils, scissors, glue, red paint, pieces of card to put it on, paint brushes, water pots, strips of white crepe paper, circles of grey sugar paper (about 10 cm diameter) charcoal and white chalk.

Talk About

- Who Florence Nightingale was, when she lived and what she was famous for.
- The uniforms worn by nurses today and where the nearest hospital is.
- What it is like in hospital today and the children's own experiences of being in or visiting a hospital.
- What it might have been like in a hospital in Florence Nightingale's time - the equipment now and then.
- What a profile is.
- Cutting shapes out of black paper.
- Making paint runny by loading a brush with water and allowing it to drip.
- The way light shines in the darkness - bright near the centre and darker towards the outside of the beam.
- Smudging chalk and charcoal together as well as leaving patches that are black and white to create different tones.

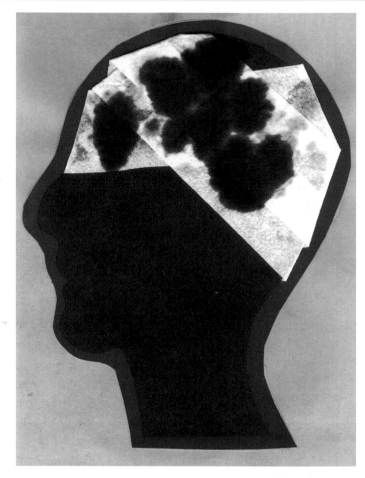

Doing

- Get a piece of black paper and use a pencil to sketch the profile of a head - use a friend as a model to help you see what a profile looks like.
- Cut this silhouette out, get some strips of crepe paper and wrap and glue them around part of your cut-out head as if they were a bandage.
- Get some red paint, some water and a brush. Load the brush with water before dipping into the paint and dripping and flicking it on to the crepe paper bandage as though it is blood!!!
- Get a circle of grey sugar paper, some charcoal and some chalk. Colour a large patch of white in the centre of the circle and a broad rim of black around the outer edge. Smudge these colours towards each other to make a band of grey between them but still leaving the original areas of black and white.

Display

Back the board with grey paper and arrange the silhouettes of the heads, on red and grey, as a border around the edge. Spray the chalk work with hair spray as a fixative before arranging the circles in a ring in the middle of the board. Add a cut out silhouette of a lamp in black to the centre of the ring. Include written work in rows in the space around it.

Observational Drawings of Older Relatives from Memory

Equipment Needed

Pieces of paper A3 size, paint, paintbrushes, pieces of card to use as mixing palettes and oil pastel crayons. A time line. Pictures and photographs of old people including the children's grandparents if possible.

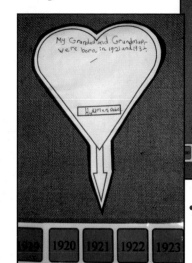

Talk About

- How the children's grandparents differ from themselves in appearance - and why - to develop an awareness of time order (old, young, long ago).
- The date of each child's birthday and the year in which they were born.
- The date of their grandparents' birthdays and the year in which they were born.
- Finding these dates on the time line and talking about the differences in the time order.
- Looking at the pictures of old people and talking about similarities and differences between them.
- Comparing their appearance with that of an older person.
- The features shown in a portrait and their position on a face.
- The colours needed and how to mix them on a card palette.
- Drawing shapes with a paintbrush before filling them in.
- Drawing and adding further details using an oil pastel.

Doing

- Get a piece of A3 paper, a paint brush and some paint on a card palette.
- Draw the outline of a face on the paper with only a finger to get an idea of the size needed to fill the paper before mixing a pale shade of paint e.g. grey to draw the same shape on the paper using a paintbrush.
- Mix the colours to fill the shape either to match a photograph or from memory.
- Add features, a neck and shoulders.
- Allow the work to dry before adding further details to it e.g. eyelashes, patterns on clothes using oil pastel crayons.

Display

Back the board with a neutral colour. Mount the paintings individually. Arrange a time line along the bottom of the board. Position the paintings over the appropriate dates on the time line. Include written work and captions by the children about their grandparents next to or below the paintings. Photographs or drawings of the children could also be added to the time line to emphasise the time order.

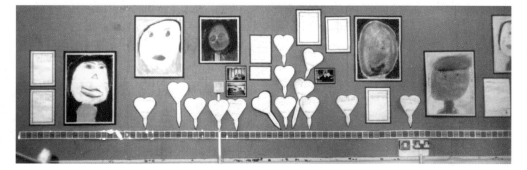

Personal History

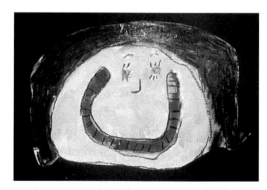

How We Look Now and How We Might Look in the Future

Equipment Needed

Mirrors, paint, paintbrushes and pieces of card for use as mixing palettes. Oil pastel crayons, wool, felt and other collage material, scissors and glue. Pieces of blue paper and white paper A3 size. Pictures of babies, toddlers, children, adults and old people including pictures of members of their own families.

Talk About

- The pictures of the people of various ages and the similarities and differences between them. How to arrange the pictures in a sequence that shows the transition stages from babies to adults.
- The changes that occur as people get older and how they themselves might change and look when they are adults.
- The features they are going to focus on and show in their portraits and the position of these features on a face. The colours needed and how to mix them.
- Cutting and sticking the different types of collage material - how much glue to use and where to put it. Drawing and adding further details with an oil pastel crayon.

Doing

- For self-portraits the children will need mirrors to look in as they work.
- Get a piece of A3 paper either white or blue, a paint brush and some pale grey paint on a card palette.
- Draw the outline of a face on the paper with a finger to get an idea of the size to fill the paper before mixing a pale shade of paint e.g. grey to draw the same shape on the paper using a paintbrush.

- Remember to look in the mirror from time to time to choose and mix the right colours to fill the shape and add the features. Use collage materials for the facial features of these self-portraits of their faces in the future. Add further details e.g. cheeks using oil pastel crayons.

Display

Mount the work individually and either arrange them as two displays or two separate blocks within a display; one of the 'Now' portraits and one of the 'Future' portraits. Or arrange them as a display of 'Now' portraits each above its matching 'Future' portrait.

Personal History

Observational Drawings of Activities Enjoyed at School

Equipment Needed
Digital photographs of different activities undertaken during the school day. Drawing pencils (4b-6b), wax crayons and pieces of white paper A4 size. Pictures of classrooms in the past, the teachers and the children at their lessons. Pictures of both old and modern school buildings. Old school photographs and school books that belonged to parents and grandparents if possible.

Talk About
- The pictures of the school buildings, whether they are similar to their own school or different. Whether they think their own school is an old or a modern building - and why.
- The furniture and equipment in the classrooms in the pictures and the furniture and equipment in their classroom - what is the same and what is different?
- The clothes the children and teachers are wearing in the pictures, how the classroom is arranged, what is on the walls and the sort of activities that they think are going on.
- The way in which school life today is different from school life in the past.
- The activities being undertaken in the digital photographs of their own school day. Those they enjoy most - and least - and why.
- Sketching lightly with a pencil the outline of shapes in a picture rather than pressing down firmly. Remembering some shapes are larger than others.
- Pressing down firmly with a wax crayon to fill the shapes with a rich covering of colour.

Doing
- Get a piece of A4 paper and a drawing pencil. When you have decided which activity you are going to draw, lightly sketch an outline of yourself doing it together with the tools and equipment you are using.
- Remember that some things in your picture need to be drawn quite big whilst others will be much smaller. Try and fill most of the paper with your drawing.
- Press down firmly with wax crayon to fill in the shapes you have drawn with lots of different colours.

Display
Mount the drawings individually and arrange them as a border around the edges of the board. Arrange the pictures of classrooms from the past as a block in the middle of the board. Add the title 'Then and Now' in the space between the two groups of work.

Food Then and Now

Equipment Needed

Paint, paintbrushes and pieces of card to use as mixing palettes. Oil pastel crayons and piece of white paper A3 in size. A selection of different types of fruit and vegetables - some whole, some cut in half.

Talk About

- The names of the different types of fruits and vegetables and whether they are grown in this country or come from another part of the world.
- Those they have tasted and those they have not.
- The shape and colour of the fruit and vegetables and what both the inside and outside look like.
- Why fruit and vegetables are good for us.
- Foods that are not good for us and why.
- The sort of foods that we now eat that are different from those our parents and grandparents ate - e.g. fast food, frozen food etc. and why we are now able to eat them- what has changed our eating habits?
- Food we like best and food we like least.
- Drawing with a paint brush on a large sheet of paper, starting with an outline before filling it in.
- Mixing the colours needed on a card palette.
- Drawing in details later using oil pastels.

Doing

- Get a piece of A3 paper and choose a vegetable or fruit from the selection.
- Look at its shape carefully before sketching it large enough to fill the paper, first with only a finger and then

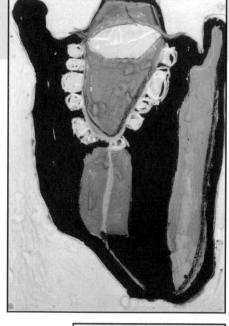

using a paint brush and a pale shade of paint e.g. grey.

- Mix the colours of paint you will need to fill the shape on a card palette with a paintbrush after looking carefully at the fruit or vegetable again.
- When you have filled in the main shapes, allow the painting to dry before drawing further details over the top using oil pastel crayons.

Display

Back the board with green paper. Mount the pieces of work individually and display them in rows with equal spaces between them across the board. Add the title 'Healthy Eating' above the display. Below the display add the title 'Unhealthy Eating' and cover a surface under the display with a collage of sweet wrappers, crisp packets etc. and pictures of foods previously discussed that are not good for us.

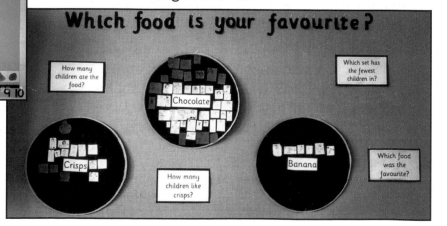

Painting a Sequence of Activities Undertaken in the Course of a Day

Equipment Needed

Paint, paint brushes, pieces of card to use as mixing palettes and white paper A3 size. Magazine pictures and story book pictures that show familiar activities e.g. breakfast time, or other normal daily routines.

Talk About

- The activities the children undertook before they came to school.
- The activities the children have undertaken so far today in school.
- The activities that are still to come in the course of the day e.g. playtime, lunchtime, hometime etc.
- The activities that the children will undertake when they get home before they go to bed.
- The fact that these ongoing activities make a sequence over the course of a day.
- Arrange the pictures in a sequence so that they fit into the pattern of a day, encouraging the use of the words before, after, soon, later, earlier etc.
- The activity from their day that has happened or is going to happen, that they are going to draw. It will need to show them doing it.
- Make sure there is going to be variety in the work i.e. that not all the children are going to paint the same thing.
- Drawing shapes with a paint brush.
- Making them large enough to fill the paper.

Doing

- Get a piece of A3 paper, a paint brush and some paint on a card palette.
- Decide which activity you are going to draw with a paint brush on your paper.
- Include yourself, furniture and the equipment you use in your chosen activity.
- Don't put too much paint on your brush or it will be difficult to draw with.
- Remember some things in your picture will be bigger than others - you will probably be the biggest.
- Make sure your picture is big enough to fill most of the paper.

Display

Divide the display board into three - before school, at school and after school. You could use three colours or just divide the board in three using border roll. Mount the work individually and place it in rows in the appropriate part of the board. Under the work in each section of the board include a list of the activities illustrated there.

Beautiful Beetles

Equipment Needed

Biros or drawing pencils, squares of yellow and/or turquoise paper 17x 17 cm approx, squares of press print similar in size and shape to the paper, black printing ink, rollers and inking trays. Gold, red and turquoise foil, gold, red and blue sequins, red, yellow and blue paper, scissors and glue. Sketch books or scrap pieces of paper for preliminary drawings. Pictures of beetles.

Talk About

- The importance of scarab beetles to the Ancient Egyptians - the scarab which takes its form from the humble dung beetle was deemed sacred because it mimicked the passage of the sun across the heavens as it struggled to roll balls of dung containing its eggs over long distances. The beetle was thought to be a form of the sun god Khepri and its ball of dung, the sun, representing new life. Scarab amulets were commonly buried with the dead as symbols of regeneration.
- The body, head, wing and leg shapes of the beetles in the pictures.
- Drawing into press print using a biro or pencil.
- How to ink up press print using a roller and a tray of printing ink.
- Pressing the inked up tile on to paper and then peeling it off to reveal an image. Adding symmetrical decoration to both halves of the image.

Doing

- Look carefully at the pictures of the beetles before sketching several beetle shapes of your own on scrap paper or in a sketch book. Choose one to copy and draw on the surface of a press print tile using either a biro or a pencil. Press firmly into the tile as you draw or the image will not print clearly.
- Put some black printing ink into a tray and

run a roller across it several times. When the roller has a good covering of ink run it across your drawing and then press the drawing onto a square of yellow or turquoise  paper. Rub the back of the paper to make sure it is pressed all over the inked up surface.

- Peel the paper away from the press print to reveal a print of your beetle. Allow it to dry before using the range of collage material to decorate your print.
- The decoration needs to be symmetrical i.e. the decoration on each side of the beetle needs to be the same.

Display

Cut a large silhouette of a beetle out of black paper to go in the centre of the board. Mount the decorated beetles onto either yellow or turquoise paper to contrast with the original colour worked on and display them in rows, with equal spaces between them, around the silhouette.

Design Based on the Eye of Horus

Equipment Needed

Pieces of white paper A4 size, pencils, black sugar paper, scissors, glue, black, red, turquoise, yellow and blue felt tip pens. Pictures that show the design of the eye of Horus.

Talk About

- In Ancient Egypt the right eye of Horus, the sky god, was his solar eye, and the left eye his 'wadjet eye' or eye of the moon. This wadjet eye symbolises the power of light and was one of the most sacred and protective charms in Egyptian magic.
- The shape of their own eyes and the shape of the eye of Horus.
- Cutting the outline shape of an eye out of black paper, removing the centre of the cut out shape leaving only an outline.
- Cutting other shapes out of black paper to fit in and go round the cut out eye shape.
- Drawing different lines and shapes using felt tip pens. Colouring in the shapes.

Doing

- Draw the outline of an eye shape on a piece of black paper - it needs to be fairly large - and cut it out. Cut the middle out of the shape leaving only a black outline. Lay it on a piece of white paper and cut an eyeball shape to go in it, and curved shapes similar to those in the pictures of the eye of Horus to go underneath it. When you are happy with the size and shape of the pieces you have cut, stick them down carefully.
- Get a black felt tip pen and, leaving a slight gap draw a line around the shape of the eye. Leave another gap before you draw a second line around the shape that is different from the first e.g. it could be wiggly,

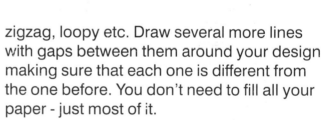

zigzag, loopy etc. Draw several more lines with gaps between them around your design making sure that each one is different from the one before. You don't need to fill all your paper - just most of it.

- Now draw - again in black - a row of matching shapes e.g. circles between the first two lines you drew. Draw a row of different matching shapes between the next two lines. Continue adding rows of different matching shapes until all the gaps have been filled. Use the other colours of felt tip pens to colour in the shapes carefully to make a richly patterned, colourful design.

Display

Photographs of the children's own eyes could form the centre of the display surrounded by rows of the patterned eyes individually mounted on black paper and with equal spaces between them.

Design and Make a 3D Crown for a Pharaoh

Equipment Needed

Newspaper, strips of white card and pieces of coloured card, a stapler, tissue paper in assorted colours, glue, scissors, foil and pieces of coloured paper, pencils, scrap paper or sketch books for preliminary work. Pictures of Pharaohs wearing a variety of different crowns.

Talk About

*   That the kings or Pharaohs in ancient Egypt had several different crowns, but each one had a serpent (or snake) at the front. The serpent was the symbol of royalty.
*   Finding examples of the different crowns - and their names - worn by the Pharaohs both in the pictures and on the Internet. The size, shape and colour of these crowns.
*   Stapling newspaper on to a strip of card, tearing tissue paper into small pieces and gluing them to overlap and cover a surface. Cutting and folding pieces of card and paper into different shapes.
*   Sketching designs for a new crown.

Doing

*   Lay several sheets of folded newspaper on top of one another on a flat surface and staple a band or strip of card to the top and bottom of the group.

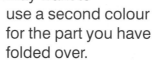

*   Join both bands together so that the newspaper now forms a tall upright tube. You may want to fold over part of the top to alter the shape slightly and add padding with crumpled newspaper to the base.

*   Look carefully at the designs in your sketches and decide which one you are going to follow. Choose a colour of tissue paper that matches one of the Egyptian crowns

in the pictures, tear it into small pieces and using glue cover the surface of your newspaper shape. Allow the pieces to overlap. You may want to use a second colour for the part you have folded over.

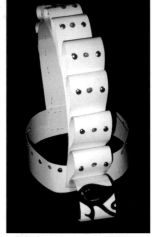

*   When the glue is dry your crown will be fairly rigid. Add further decoration to it using the different papers and foil. Remember to match the colours to those of actual crowns. Decorate the sides and the back as well as the front and remember where you need to include a snake.
*   As an alternative, strips of card stapled together and decorated create a simple crown shape.

Display

The crowns could be displayed on a flat surface covered with black or blue paper in front of a board on which there is information about actual crowns, the designs the children drew and photographs of them making their crowns. Alternatively they could be displayed on shelves, made from boxes, attached to the board - (see the book Display in the Primary School page 28.)

Printing a Design for an Ancient Egyptian Collar

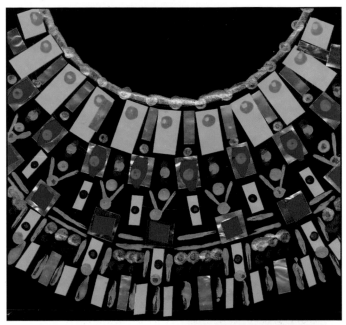

Equipment Needed

Squares of black sugar paper 21 x 21 cm approx, red, yellow and turquoise paint and foil, pieces of card to put the paint on, scissors, glue, cotton buds, thin strips of card and other reclaimed materials to use for printing pictures of Egyptian collars.

Talk About

*   The Ancient Egyptians were lovers of fashion and beauty. They went to great lengths to adorn themselves with cosmetics, wigs and jewellery. Wide bead collars were popular; these had broad bands of repeating colours and were often decorated with claws, horns, tusks and shells as well as stone beads.
*   The colours, materials and stones that were popular in Egyptian jewellery - Carnelian (blood red), Turquoise (blue green), Lapis Lazuli (blue), Jasper (red, yellow or brown quartz), Garnet (red) Amethyst (purple) Gold and Silver.
*   The shape of the complete collars and the arrangement of the shapes and repeating patterns on the collars in the pictures. Where the largest shapes and smallest shapes are positioned.
*   The shapes that can be printed by dipping the reclaimed materials in paint before pressing them on to paper.
*   Printing shapes on top of and inside each other as well as next to and above and below each other.
*   Cutting shapes of different sizes out of coloured paper - folding the paper first so that there are several versions of the same shape.

Doing

*   Get a piece of card and put the different colours of paint on it. Get a square of black paper and the reclaimed materials you want to use.

*   Dip the edge of a strip of card into one of the colours of paint and use it to print a curve (semi-circle) at the top of the paper to start the shape of the collar. Use the different reclaimed materials in turn to print rows of repeated shapes under each other following the shape of the original curve but getting wider each time.

*   Once the basic shape and design has been completed add further decoration to it with more printing (on top of shapes and inside shapes) and shapes cut from the different coloured papers and foil. Use all the different colours of paint.
*   See Step by Step Art Book 6 page 66 for computer generated collar designs.

Display

Mount the work individually on gold or red and display it in equally spaced rows around a central title on a board backed with black or blue paper.

Patterns Using Ancient Egyptian Motifs

Equipment Needed

Strips of black paper 8cm in width, A4 in length, pieces of cream paper 21x15 cm, glue, scissors, pencils, red, gold, blue and turquoise paper and foil. Examples of patterns that use Ancient Egyptian motifs.

Talk About

- The Egyptians relied for inspiration on the natural world for their decorative motifs. Many motifs were developed from plants which played an important role in their lives. They were based on observation but took on conventional forms when they appeared and were repeated in Egyptian designs. The most popular plant forms were Papyrus, Lotus, Garlands, Spiral Scrolls and Lilies.
- Finding examples of these motifs in the Egyptian patterns.
- Copying some of these shapes and decorating them to form a new repeating pattern.
- Folding a strip of paper in half and then in half again.
- Drawing on it a motif that touches the top and bottom of the strip as well as both sides.
- Cutting the motif out whilst the paper is folded - remembering to leave a hinge at each end, so that when the strip is opened up the motifs remain joined together to form a repeating pattern.
- Cutting similar shapes of different sizes to decorate the motifs.

Doing

- Get a strip of black paper, fold it in half and then in half again before drawing an Ancient Egyptian motif on it in pencil. Cut the motif out whilst the paper is still folded, keeping a hinge at each end! When you open the strip you should have a row of repeating motifs to stick down across your piece of cream paper which needs to be placed portrait way up.

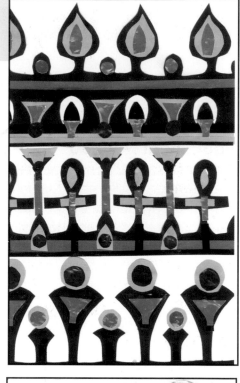

- Get another strip of black paper, fold it in the same way as the first but draw a different Ancient Egyptian motif on it. Cut it out and stick it across the cream paper in the same way leaving a gap between it and the first row of motifs.

- Continue in the same way until you have several rows of different repeated motifs with gaps between them across your paper. Cut shapes from the coloured paper and foils to decorate these motifs. Remember each motif in a row must be decorated in the same way to keep the repeated pattern.

Display

Mount the repeated patterns on red or turquoise paper and use them as a border around the edge of a board on which there is written work about the Ancient Egyptians.

Greek Key Pattern on a Mosaic Background

Equipment Needed

Strips of paper 2/3 cm wide in yellow and orange. Strips of a similar width in copper and gold foil. Thin strips of black paper about 1 cm wide, glue and scissors. Squares of brown sugar paper 21x 21 cm and pictures that show examples of both the Greek Key pattern and also of mosaics.

Talk About

*   What the Greek Key pattern looks like and where it is found in the pictures.
*   Why it is called a Key pattern - because 'key' means 'meander' in Greek. A meander is a continuous winding pattern that keeps turning on itself.
*   What a mosaic is and where they appear in the pictures. Mosaics are patterns made with hundreds of tiny squares of coloured glass, pebbles, gold or marble. Ancient Greek artists invented mosaic pictures. At first they were made only on floors, but later wall mosaics were made as well.
*   Finding examples of mosaics and the Greek Key pattern using the Internet.
*   Making straight cuts across strips of paper to produce squares and rectangles.
*   Cutting black strips into shorter pieces and arranging them to make one of the repeating shapes found in the Greek Key pattern.

Doing

*   Get a square of brown sugar paper to use as a background and some of the cut strips of coloured paper and foil.
*   Make straight cuts across the strips to produce small squares and rectangles.

*   Glue these shapes closely together with only small gaps between them in rows across the brown sugar paper. You may need to get more strips to cut up as you work.
*   Mix the coloured papers up as you work so that there is plenty of variety of colour in each row.
*   When the background is full, get some of the thin cut strips of black paper, cut them into shorter lengths and arrange them to make one of the repeating shapes that make up the Greek Key pattern in the middle of your mosaic.
*   Only stick the strips down when you are happy with the shape they make.

Display

Unmounted these individual pieces of work could be arranged closely together to form a border around a board on which there is written work and information about the Ancient Greeks.

Menacing Medusa

Equipment Needed

Clay, either grey or terracotta cut into individual pieces. Paper towel or clay boards to rest the clay on whilst working so that it does not stick to the table top. Scissors, pipe cleaners and sandwich bag ties (long versions of these are available from TTS - Technology Teaching Systems, Monk Road, Alfreton, Derbyshire) and an assortment of wiggly eyes. The story of Medusa - and other Greek Myths.

Talk About

*   What a Myth is - a story about the gods and superhuman beings. A popular pastime in ancient Greece was telling stories. The Greeks made up exciting tales about the gods, and about heroes who defeated magical monsters. At first, Greek myths were passed on by word of mouth, later they were written down by poets and playwrights such as Hesiod and Euripides.
*   The story of Medusa, why she became a monster and what happened to her in the end.
*   Other Greek Myths e.g. Jason and the Golden Fleece, the Minotaur.
*   How to roll clay into a ball and how to pull and prod shapes in clay.
*   The shape of writhing snakes.
*   Twisting pipe cleaners and sandwich ties into twisted spirals.
*   What makes a face appear frightening or ugly.

Doing

*   Get a piece of clay and lay it on a paper towel or clay board. Now roll it into a ball, then with your eyes closed - no cheating! - begin to model it into a face. Pull out shapes for the ears, the nose and chin and press in

hollows for the eyes and mouth. Open your eyes and see what you have created. Work on and add to or change some of the features you have made if you wish.

*   Get two wiggly eyes and press them into the eye sockets.
*   Twist and curl some pipe cleaners before pressing

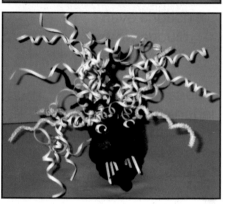

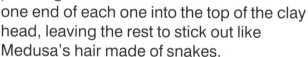

one end of each one into the top of the clay head, leaving the rest to stick out like Medusa's hair made of snakes.
*   Bend or cut a pipe cleaner into smaller pieces using scissors and press these into the mouth shape to represent teeth. If you make them crooked and allow them to protrude they will look really ugly.

Display

Arrange the Medusa heads on a covered flat surface in front of a board. Display a picture of Medusa and the myth about her on the board. Add other Greek myths as well if there is space.

Using the Colours of Greek Vases for Pattern Work

Equipment Needed

Thin wax crayons or felt tip pens, 'Polar graph' maths paper - found in most educational catalogues. Black sugar paper (A4 size), pencils, scissors and pictures of Greek vases showing a variety of shapes and sizes. Strips of gold foil.

Talk About

- The different shapes and sizes of the Greek vases, the names of some of the vases and what they were used for e.g. amphorae were used for storing wine.
- The colours of the vases - artists painted patterns and pictures on red clay pots with a mixture of clay water and ash. They scratched details into the clay with a pointed tool leaving the background red. Pots were then fired in a kiln which made them turn black until they were exposed to air, then the painted parts stayed black and the rest turned red. In about 510 BC the red figure style took over, this method was similar to the previous one but this time the background was black and the figures appeared red.
- The pictures and patterns on the vases - the pictures were often scenes from daily life and Greek myths. Usually there was a different picture on each side, but sometimes the scene carried on right round the vase. Patterns appear above and below the scenes, around the neck, base and handles.
- Finding crayons or felt tip pens that match the colours of the Greek vases.
- Colouring carefully inside the spaces on the 'polar graph' paper.
- Cutting shapes out of a folded piece of black paper keeping the fold intact.

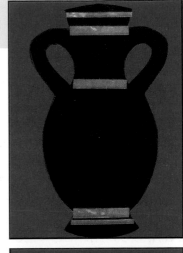

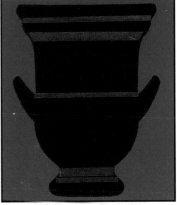

Doing

- Get a piece of 'polar graph' paper, a pencil and the terracotta and black drawing media you are going to use. Mark out faintly with a pencil on the 'polar graph' paper the shapes that you are going to fill in with each of the two colours. When filled these should form a pattern. Colour firmly and deeply and make sure each shape is completely filled. Take care to keep inside the lines.
- Get a piece of black sugar paper; fold it in half and on it in pencil draw half of a Greek vase. The outside shape of the vase is on the outside of the paper. Cut the shape out carefully whilst the paper is folded then open it up to reveal a complete vase. Add bands of decoration using strips of gold foil.

Display

Mount the patterns individually on black paper. Back the board with a terracotta colour. Arrange the pictures of Greek vases in the centre surrounded by a border made up of the patterns. Arrange the silhouettes of the vases around the outer edge of the display on orange and brown squares.

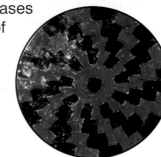

Comedy and Tragedy Cut Paper Faces

Equipment Needed

Large pieces of black sugar paper, strips of black paper and small pieces of white paper, scissors, white oil pastels, pictures of faces showing happy and sad expressions including Ancient Greek theatre masks.

Talk About

- The fact that the Ancient Greeks loved to go to the theatre. Plays were performed during religious festivals and even the poorest people were able to go. Some plays written by Greek dramatists are still performed today. In the plays there was a chorus and only a few actors who played all the parts. The actors wore masks which showed whether their characters were comic or tragic. All actors were men, so if there was a woman in the play an actor would wear a mask to make him look like a woman.
- What a comedy is and what a tragedy is.
- Which of the faces in the pictures look comic and which look tragic and how the features change in each case.
- Making comic faces and tragic faces - these could be recorded using a digital camera for use in the final display.
- Cutting a shape out of a folded piece of paper keeping the fold intact.
- Curling strips of paper and making zigzag folds along strips of paper.
- Drawing with oil pastel crayons - they are soft and break easily.

Doing

- Get a piece of black paper and fold it in half lengthways. Keep the paper folded whilst you draw the outline of a face on it with an oil pastel. The middle of your face is where the fold is. Cut out the face shape, draw an eye shape on the folded face and cut this shape

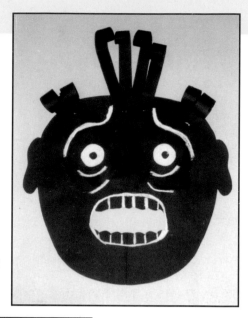

out. Open the paper to reveal two eyes on a full face.
- Keep the paper open and draw in a nose and mouth. Cut out the mouth.

The type of features you have chosen to draw should make your face look either happy or sad. Use white paper to add details e.g. to fill in eye sockets, add teeth etc.

- Add hair using the strips of paper folded or curled.
- Draw and outline details on your face to make it look either happier or sadder.

Display

- Mount photographs of the children making comic and tragic faces and arrange them as a block in the middle of the board. Arrange the comic and tragic masks around the outside of the block.

Printing Acanthus Leaves and Making Decorative Pillars

Equipment Needed

Strips of black sugar paper, scissors, pencils, press print, white printing ink, rollers and inking trays. Broad strips of paper, white paper, corrugated paper, white card, art straws, pipe cleaners and glue. Pictures of Greek pillars decorated in a variety of ways i.e. plain ones and those with acanthus leaves and swirls and Greek temples.

Doing

- Get a piece of press print and with a pencil draw the shape of a spiky leaf on it. Cut the leaf shape out; ink it up using a roller covered with white ink from the inking tray. Take a strip of black sugar paper and press the inked up leaf on it several times to produce a row of repeating prints.

- Get a broad strip of black paper and trim it into the shape of a pillar.
- Use card or paper to add detail up the length of the pillar as in the pictures before deciding on the decorative style it should have at the top e.g. swirls using pipe cleaners or paper curls or cut out spiky leaves. Choose the materials you feel are most appropriate to achieve your design.

Talk About

- The style of important Greek buildings e.g. temples - these buildings were designed to be as elegantly shaped as possible and this approach has inspired architects throughout the ages. The idea of building as an art form came from the Greeks. Another idea was that the key to the beauty of a building was in its measurements. Important Greek buildings had imposing groups of pillars, which were decorated at the top (the capital) in a variety of styles. The Doric style was plain, the Ionic style had swirls and the Corinthian style had carvings in the shape of prickly acanthus leaves.

- Finding information and illustrations about Ancient Greek buildings on the Internet.

- Drawing shapes into press print and cutting them out and inking up a shape using a roller and printing ink. How to print the shape.

- Cutting the shape of a pillar out of paper and decorating it to make it appear in a 'Greek' style.

Display

Arrange the printed strips of Acanthus leaves along the top and bottom of the board and the individual pillars as a border down the sides. Use some pillars to decorate a 3D temple made from two boxes of equal size. Display this below the board and fill the centre of the board with written work and material from the Internet about Ancient Greek buildings.

Magnificent Masks

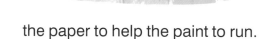

Equipment Needed

Strips of paper in different shades of blue, white paper (A3 size), oil pastel crayons, black paper, black felt tip pens, turquoise paint, paintbrushes, pieces of card as palettes, water pots, large pieces of card to rest the paper on, paper clips to attach it and newspaper to cover the table. A picture of the turquoise mask of Quetzalcoatl.

Talk About

- Aztecs believed in many gods and goddesses who created and controlled the world and kept the sun moving across the sky. To thank the gods and keep them happy Aztec priests gave them human sacrifices. This mask of the god Quetzalcoatl is made of turquoise with white shell eyes and teeth. Turquoise was highly valued and was often used in representations of gods or tied to weapons to ensure accuracy.
- Fastening a piece of white paper on to a piece of card with a paper clip, tilting the card so the paint will run down it. Loading a brush with a lot of water as well as paint, so the mixture will run down the paper.
- Cutting strips of paper into small pieces and filling in the spaces outlined by the paint.
- Colouring with oil pastel crayons. Outlining shapes with a black felt pen.

Doing

- Fasten a piece of A3 paper to a piece of card, tilt the card and run a paint brush loaded with blue paint and water along the top of the paper. Encourage the paint to run down the paper as far as possible by tilting the card further. Run a second brush loaded with water only on top of

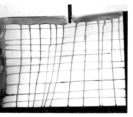

the paper to help the paint to run.
- Repeat this along each of the sides of the paper in turn by refastening it to the card and turning it to allow the paint to run down it and creating an irregular grid as the runs of paint meet and cross over.
- Allow the grid to dry. Cut it into the shape of the mask and fill in the spaces on it with shapes cut from the strips of the various blue papers. Colour in some of the spaces as well using oil pastel crayons in shades of blue. Add eyes, a mouth and teeth using black and white paper. Outline them with a black pen.

Display

Arrange the masks in rows around the edge of a board. Display a copy of the original in the centre of the board surrounded by the children's written descriptions of the methods they used to make their masks. Add information about Aztec masks found on the Internet.

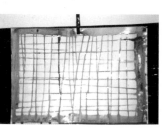

Fancy Feathers

Equipment Needed
Long strips of white card (5cm in width), art straws, masking tape, crepe paper - rainbow crepe paper works particularly well - pipe cleaners, scissors, glue and coloured feathers.

Talk About
- That the Aztecs fashioned elaborate feathered headdresses to wear. Glue made from the resin of rubber trees was used for attaching the feathers to a frame made of reeds or light wood. War shields were decorated with feathers too. Feathers were one of the most important articles to be delivered up to the tax collectors in the Aztec empire.
- Other cultures for whom feathered headdresses are important e.g. North American Indians, African tribes.
- How feathers are still used today to decorate ceremonial head wear and ladies hats etc.
- The different colours, sizes and shapes of the feathers to be used.
- Sticking them on to a background, threading them between strips and pushing them into holes when making a headdress.
- Cutting crepe paper into strips and fringing some of the strips.

Doing
- Get a strip of card, masking tape and some art straws. Lay the strip of card flat on a surface and along it arrange art straws extending upwards from the card, but still lying on the flat surface. Allow a small equal gap between each straw. Fasten the straws to the card with masking tape.

- Fasten the ends of the card together with masking tape - allowing the straws to stand upright. Gather the straws together - at the top or half way up and fasten the group together using a pipe cleaner to make a framework.
- Decorate this framework by sticking strips of crepe paper to it, weaving strips through it, tying strips to it etc. Add feathers to various parts of it by threading, weaving and gluing them to the framework and pushing them into the open ends of the art straws.
- Children with allergies to feathers could cut feather shapes out of coloured paper to combine with the crepe paper.

Display
Arrange the headdresses on a flat surface covered with black paper. The board behind this display could be decorated using the activity described on the next page or with photographs of the children both constructing and wearing their headdresses.

Draw and Create a New Aztec God

Equipment Needed

Pieces of white paper A3 size, pieces of black paper and strips of black paper, pieces of coloured paper, scissors, glue and foil. Black felt tip pens and pictures of Aztec gods. Sketchbooks or scrap paper and pencils for preliminary work.

Talk About

- That the Aztecs believed in many gods who created and controlled the world and kept the sun moving across the sky. The Aztecs recognised images of their gods by their special clothing, elaborate headdresses, ornaments, face decoration and the objects they held e.g. Tezcatlipoca - god of warriors, the night sky and thieves had black striped face paint and a mirror as part of his headdress. Chalchiuhtlicue - the goddess of the waters had a green feathered headdress and Chicomecoatl - the goddess of ripe maize had a rectangular shaped headdress with streamers and tassles. To thank the gods and keep them happy Aztec priests gave them human sacrifices.
- Finding out about more Aztec gods using the Internet.
- Drawing a shape on black paper, and cutting the centre out of it leaving just a black outline. Using strips cut into different lengths and shapes to divide up the inside of the outline.
- Drawing a design for a fantastic headdress. Including in the design shapes that will inform the onlooker as to the role of this new god.

Doing

- On a piece of black paper draw the shape of a head in profile - it could be your own profile if the overhead projector is used to project a shadow of your profile on to paper pinned to

the wall. Cut this shape out, fold it to make a cut in it and then remove the middle of the shape leaving just an outline.
- Stick this on to a piece of white paper and use the black paper strips and the black felt tip pens to add eyes, lips, teeth, hair, decoration and detail to the face.
- Draw in pencil the outline of the headdress your god is going to wear on top of their head. Cut the coloured paper and foil into shapes and use it to build up and decorate the headdress and remember to include shapes on the headdress that tell us the role of your god.
- Add an Aztec style name for your god typed up using the computer.

Display

Mount the work individually on black and then red paper. Display each one complete with its Aztec name in rows across a board backed in grey.

Eye Catching Eagles

Equipment Needed
Scissors, glue, pieces of black paper, squares of orange paper 25 x 25 cm approx, pictures of eagles, vultures and hawks and Aztec designs featuring eagles. A sketch book or scrap paper and pencils for preliminary work.

Talk About
- To the Aztecs the eagle symbolised the rising sun and celestial power. It was associated with the warrior clans and jewellery in the shape of an eagle head was often worn as protection. The Aztecs believed that the god Huitzilopochtli told them to find the spot where an eagle stood on a cactus holding a snake. Here they would build a city and become great rulers. It was here that the Aztec city of Tecnochtitlan was built.
- Finding Aztec designs featuring eagles using the Internet.
- Collecting information in a series of rough sketches i.e. eye shapes, beaks, head shapes, feathers etc. concentrating on outline shapes rather than detail.
- Looking at how the Aztec designs fit together with gaps between the pieces.
- Cutting shapes out of black paper.

Doing
- Get a square of orange paper and some black paper.
- On the black paper draw some of the shapes you are going to use for your eagles head and cut them out carefully. Use the sketches you made for ideas.

- Start by creating the outline of the head, then the eye, beak etc.
- You may find that removing the inside of some shapes leaving just an outline is effective.
- Putting smaller shapes inside the outline of a shape or cutting shapes in half and moving them slightly apart creates an interesting effect.
- Arrange the shapes on the orange background leaving gaps between the pieces. They need to be quite big and bold and to fill most of the paper. Cut larger versions of your shapes if you feel your first ones are not big enough.
- Stick these shapes down carefully before cutting further shapes from the black paper to complete your design.

Display
Back the board with black paper. Put the information found on the Internet about Aztecs and eagle designs on black then orange paper in the centre of the board. Mount the cut out eagle heads on black and arrange them in rows as a border around the edge of the board.

Ferocious Faces

Equipment Needed

Pieces of black, orange, brown and grey paper, brass paper fasteners, wiggly eyes, glue and scissors. Pictures of helmeted Viking warriors.

Talk About

- Who the Vikings were, where they came from and where they landed in Britain - the Viking homelands were in Scandinavia, they were tremendous travellers, raiding, conquering or settling in many European lands as well as trading goods far and wide. Vikings were superb sailors and shipbuilders, their most famous vessels were the speedy longships used on raiding voyages. Viking warriors fought with bows and arrows, battle axes and spears but their favourite weapon was a double edged sword. A Viking raider would wear a loose fitting woollen shirt and trousers, topped with a chain mail or padded tunic, woollen socks and leather shoes. On his head he would wear a helmet of metal and leather. This might have had eye and nose guards but no horns. Vikings wore long hair and long moustaches or neatly trimmed beards.
- The features of the Vikings in the pictures.
- Cutting half a face shape out of a folded piece of paper keeping the fold intact.
- Cutting paper into broad and narrow strips. Shaping strips to look like eye masks. Curling and fringing thin paper strips.
- Cutting large holes (for the eyes to look through) in a strip of paper.

Doing

- Get a piece of grey paper, fold it in half and cut the shape of half a face from it. The centre of the face will be along the fold. Open the cut shape to reveal a complete face.
- Get a piece of black paper and cut the shape of a helmet from it - it needs to be the right

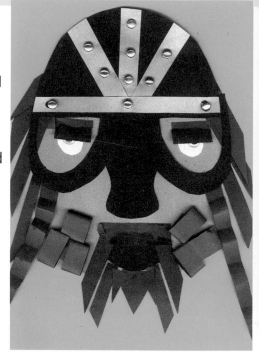

size to fit on top of the head.
- Cut a shaped eye guard (with two holes in it) and if desired a nose guard from a strip of black or grey paper and attach them to the helmet. Add strips of grey paper to decorate the helmet pierced at intervals with brass paper fasteners.
- Add wiggly eyes to the eye holes and cut the other features - nose and mouth - out of brown paper. Stick these on the face before cutting orange paper

into thin strips, fringing and curling it to use as e.g. eyebrows, moustaches and beards.

Display

Display these unmounted faces as the border around a board on which there is written work about the Vikings.

Runic Riddles

Equipment Needed

A computer graphics programme that has a grid tool and a line tool - Dazzle has been used here. Pieces of white paper A3 size, thin strips of coloured paper, paint, pieces of card to use as palettes, sponges, draught excluder (the sponge strip variety), aerosol lids, glue, scissors, rulers and oil pastel crayons. Examples of the Runic Alphabet.

Talk About

*   What the Runic Alphabet is - Viking letters were known as runes. Each rune is formed from straight lines and diagonal lines, making it very easy to carve on wood or stone. Most surviving runic inscriptions exist on stone monuments known as rune stones. The word rune comes from the Gothic word meaning secret. Runes were shrouded in mystery because very few people could read or understand them and each rune may have had several meanings.
*   What a diagonal line is and what a vertical line is. The shape of the letters in the Runic alphabet - those that are vertical and those that are both vertical and diagonal. The shape of letters in our own alphabet.
*   The tools to use on the computer - where to find them and how to get them.
*   Printing with a sponge dipped in paint. Making letters on an aerosol lid using draught excluder and printing them. Drawing straight lines with a ruler and oil pastels.

Doing

*   When using the computer, click on the colour black then on the grid tool and then the line tool using the left-hand mouse button. Decide which letters you are going to use and repeat to make a pattern - choose only two or three and draw rows of them using the line tool and the grid. To stop

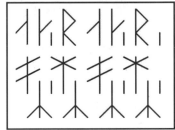 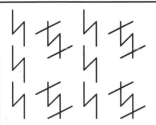

drawing a line click the right-hand mouse button and to start a new line, click as before using the left-hand mouse button. Print out your pattern when it is complete.

*   Get a piece of A3 paper, choose a colour of paint, put it on a piece of card and with a sponge print and cover the paper with colour. Using a sponge should add a texture. Get some strips of coloured paper and cut them into the length you need to make some of the letters from your pattern. Stick them on to the background. Make other letters out of draught excluder on aerosol lids and print them next to and among your collage letters. They should be smaller in size. Use oil pastel crayons and rulers to draw and add further letters.

Display

Put a print - out of the Runic alphabet in the centre of the board. Surround it with rows of the individually mounted mixed media work. Use the black and white computer work as an outer border.

Dreadful Dragons

Equipment Needed

White paper, brown and black wax crayons, brown and black papers, tissue, felt and vivelle, red and yellow felt, silver foil, brown corrugated paper, squares of grey sugar paper 22 x 22cm, scissors and glue. Pictures of dragons. Scrap paper or sketchbooks to use for initial drawings.

Talk About

*   The links between dragons and the Vikings - figureheads carved in the shape of dragons were used to decorate the prows of Viking longships. These fierce creatures were thought to bring the sailors good fortune and strike fear into their enemies. Some longships were given names such as, 'Black Raven' and 'Dragon of the Sea' after their figureheads.
*   The shape, features and expressions on the faces of the dragons in the pictures.
*   How to take a rubbing using wax crayons and paper on top of textured surfaces. Pressing down firmly to get deep colours
*   Making sketches of different dragon features to select from and use in a final design.
*   How to cut, tear and fold the different collage materials.

Doing

*   Make a sketch on scrap paper of a dragon's head using information from the preliminary sketches you made.
*   Use both black and brown crayons to take a number of different rubbings from a variety of different surfaces. Press on firmly to get a dense covering of colour and to reveal the different textures.
*   Get a square of grey sugar paper and on it roughly and lightly sketch the outline shape of your dragon's head - no details are

necessary at this stage. Make sure the sketch uses most of the space on the paper.
*   Collect and select from the collage materials and rubbings those you want to use. Cut, tear, fold and arrange the materials on your grey paper to make the main shapes of your design. When you are happy with the arrangement, stick the pieces down carefully.
*   Cut and tear and fold smaller pieces to add details to your design - remember it needs to look fierce and frightening!!

Display

Mount the pieces of work individually and arrange them in rows around the black silhouette of a complete longboat in the middle of the board.

Clever Knots

Equipment Needed

Wool, pipe cleaners or waxworks (available from YPO), squares of white paper 22 x 22cm, sponges, paint, pieces of card as palettes, scissors, pencils, glue and oil pastel crayons. Pictures of knotwork.

Talk About

- Where the Celts came from - they came from central Europe and spread in all directions until they encountered and fought the Romans. They ended up in Ireland, Scotland, Cornwall, Brittany and the Isle of Man. All Celts shared the same language, legends and customs.

- What Celtic knotwork looks like and where it is found - knotwork is the name given to the interlaced patterns used by the Celts to decorate graphic work such as manuscripts and stone monuments.

- How to plait with wool - first with three strands and then with six.
- Printing with a sponge and drawing with oil pastel crayons

- Drawing a shape on a folded piece of paper, cutting it out and cutting a central hole in it whilst keeping the two sides of the paper together.

Doing

- Choose the colours and number of strands of either pipe cleaners or waxworks you are going to work with and twist them together at one end. Plait the strands together loosely

until all of each strand has been used. Twist the ends together before stretching some of the plaited strands outwards to change shape and form holes to make the final result resembling Celtic knotwork.

- Get a square of white paper, some paint and a sponge. Dip the sponge in the paint and cover the square with printed colour. Print a second square in a contrasting colour. Allow this to dry before folding it in half and drawing on it an oval shape with a point at both ends. Cut this shape out, whilst the two pieces of paper are still on top of each other. Lay one shape on top of the first printed background and cut the other shape in half. Arrange this to thread both under and over parts of the first shape to give the appearance of a knotwork design. Stick the shapes down carefully. Add spirals and swirls to both the shapes and the background using oil pastel crayons.

Display

Attach the plaited work to a panel in the centre of the board, around pictures of knotwork designs. Mount the printed work individually and display it in rows around the edge.

Symmetrical Scabbards

Equipment Needed
Broad strips of white paper (15 x 30 cm), thick black felt tip pens, glue, scissors and papers in assorted colours including coloured foil. Pencils and scrap pieces of paper or sketchbooks for initial sketches.

Talk About
- What a scabbard is and what symmetrical means.
- Celtic artists had a wealth of motifs from which to choose for their designs - in particular they used spirals, scrolls and 'S' shapes. In pagan times spiral and 'S' shaped symbols were associated with sky and solar cults. The 'S' was rarely used singly. Symmetrical designs were the decoration often found on their scabbards and swords.
- What spiral shapes and scroll shapes look like. Drawing spiral shapes, scroll shapes and 'S' shapes of different sizes in pencil on scrap pieces of paper.
- Cutting similar shapes out of coloured paper.

Doing
- Get a piece of white paper and a black felt tip pen. Fold the paper in half lengthways and then open it up to reveal a central line. Draw a pattern of shapes and lines including spirals, 'S' shapes and scrolls on either side down the length of this centre fold. Remember the pattern must be symmetrical so that what is drawn on one side of the fold is mirrored on the opposite side.
- Work from the top of the paper downwards to avoid smudging.
- Get a second piece of white paper. Fold it in half lengthways and then open it out to reveal a central line. Chose two or three colours of paper only (including foil) and from these papers cut similar shapes to

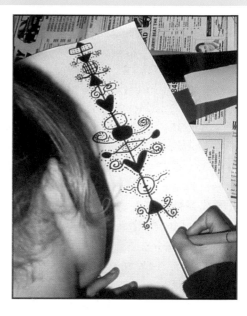

those you have drawn. Remember you will need two of each shape so that when you stick the shapes on either side of the fold the pattern will again be symmetrical.

- Arrange the shapes down the fold. Allow some of the shapes to overlap, to sit on top of larger shapes or go next to and extend other shapes to make your pattern more interesting. When you are happy with your arrangement and you have checked that the pattern is symmetrical, stick the shapes down carefully.
- Add further symmetrical lines and dots to your design using the black felt tip.

Display

Cut out the silhouette of a sword and a scabbard from black paper and arrange them in the centre of the display board. Mount the line drawings individually on black and arrange them in rows around the silhouette. Mount the collages individually and arrange them in rows as a border around the edge of the board.

Laborious Letters

Equipment Needed
Coloured felt tip pens, black card, coloured papers, gold foil, glue, scissors, squares of white paper (15 x 15 cm approx). Sketchbooks or scrap pieces of paper and pencils for initial work. Examples of illuminated letters.

Talk About
- That from the end of Roman rule to the reign of Alfred the Great, monasteries were the focus of new found Christianity and learning in Britain. Anglo-Saxon monks made beautiful handwritten books on parchment - vellum - made from animal skins. They wrote using quill pens made from stiff birds' feathers and decorated some of the letters using bright colours and gold leaf. The two most important centres for manuscript production were monasteries in Ireland and Northumberland.
- The designs that decorated the letters were often strange animals and faces with intricate patterns woven around them.
- Finding further examples of illuminated letters using the Internet.
- The ways that illuminated letters are decorated, what the designs look like and how they fit round the shapes of the letters.
- Drawing large letter shapes and cutting them out.
- Drawing initial ideas of patterns, animals and faces to select from and combined in a final design around a letter.

Doing
- Draw a large letter shape in pencil on black card - it needs to be nearly as big as the

square of white paper on which it is going to sit. Cut the letter shape out and lay it on the white paper.
- Cut shapes and strips out of coloured paper and fit them around, through and over the letter shape. When you are happy with your design stick both the letter and the shapes down carefully keeping your design intact.
- Add further detail to your design by drawing using felt tip pens and finally pieces of gold foil.
- Illuminated letters can also be designed using the computer. (See Step by Step Art 6 page 69.)

Display
Mount the pieces of work individually on black paper. Arrange them in rows around information about illuminated letters on a display board backed in red paper. Add a gold foil and black paper border around the edge of the board.

Jewellery in a Jiffy

Equipment Needed

Black, gold and silver card, black biros, pencils, single hole punches, brass paper fasteners, thread, circular shapes of different sizes to draw round, scissors and pictures of Anglo-Saxon style jewellery.

Talk About

- The fact that in the 4th and 5th centuries, jewellery was a sign of status and wealth. Kings commissioned gorgeous jewels to reward their warriors for bravery in battle. When rich people died their jewellery and favourite possessions were buried beside them.

- Jewellery was made in a variety of ways e.g. by casting, impressing, embossing, stamping or punching, inlaying and filigree. Finding out what these words mean and finding examples of Anglo-Saxon jewellery using the Internet.

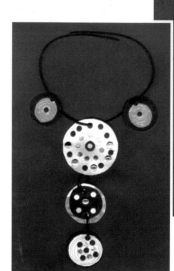

- Drawing round circular shapes and cutting them out.
- Drawing patterns into foil using a biro on the reverse side.
- Using a single hole punch to make a pattern of holes in and around a shape.
- Threading shapes together so that they hang like a necklace or pendant.

Doing

- Get some pieces of silver or gold card, a pencil, some circular shapes and a pair of scissors.
- Draw round several circular shapes of different sizes and cut them out. Arrange them to form the shape of your necklace or pendant on a flat surface.
- Decide where the holes will need to be punched in the shapes so that they can be threaded together. Use a hole punch to make the holes before threading them on a piece of cord or string.
- Further shapes could now be drawn and added on top of, or hanging from some of the threaded shapes using black card as well as the silver or gold card.
- Decorate the shapes by punching holes in them, drawing spirals and curved lines on them using a biro and pushing paper fasteners through some of them.

Display

Cut silhouettes of heads out of black paper. Arrange them in a row - or several rows - across the board. Hang the necklaces and pendants around the necks of the silhouettes to make it appear as though they are wearing them. Bracelets could be made as well and displayed round cut out hand shapes.

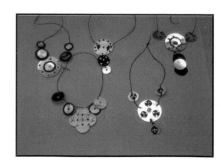

Clay Models of Imaginary Emperors

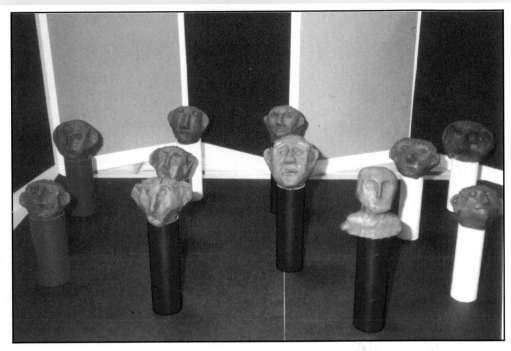

Equipment Needed

Terracotta or grey clay cut into chunks, paper towels or clay cloths to put under the clay to stop it sticking to the table top, spatulas, lolly sticks and plastic straws. Pictures of statues of Roman Emperors.

Talk About

- Where and why statues were put on display by the Romans. Sculptors and stonemasons were hired to make statues for both public buildings and private villas. Statues were brightly painted and were often of gods and goddesses as well as real people. There was a great demand also for commemorative statues. These were placed in public squares, halls or temples. Some were put on top of commemorative columns. Most were of Emperors and other important people, symbolising victory and power.
- Where they have seen statues or where there are statues in the locality and what they commemorate.
- Rolling clay into a ball. Pulling and prodding shapes out of the ball whilst still keeping it intact.
- Carving, indenting and adding texture and pattern to the clay using, spatulas and plastic straws.

Doing

- Get a chunk of clay and put it on a paper towel or clay cloth and roll the clay into a ball.
- Close your eyes, put your hands on the ball of clay and work on it with your fingers without being able to see the end result.
- Work by touch only and start pulling and pressing the features found on a face into the ball of clay. Consider and feel the position of these features, as you work e.g. eyes, nose, chin, mouth ears etc.
- Open your eyes and look at what you have modelled so far - you will probably be quite surprised with the character you have created. Use the lolly sticks, spatulas and plastic straws to add details e.g. eye balls, nostrils, eyebrows, hair (think of the hairstyles that were popular with the Romans).
- Use your fingers to do more pulling and prodding to some of the features if you think it is necessary.

Display

Arrange each of the completed heads on its own individual cardboard tube if possible on a flat surface. Ask the children to think of a Roman name for the character they have made and to type and print it out using the computer. This can then be placed under their statue.

Mosaics on a Common Theme

Equipment Needed

Squares of black sugar paper (18 x 18 cm approx), glue, pieces of red and yellow paper, pencils and scrap paper or sketch books for preliminary sketches and initial ideas.

Talk About

- What a mosaic is and how they were made - mosaics became popular from the first century A.D. They were pictures or patterns made from small pieces of coloured glass or stone. They decorated walls and floors. Artists first drew the design for a mosaic before spreading wet plaster over a small area of the floor or wall and smoothing it down before pressing the pieces of stone into it following their design. Patterns in black and white were the most common at first, and these were very fashionable around Rome. Further afield more colourful mosaics became popular. Companies of artists designed mosaics in their workshops, people chose a design then the mosaic artist came to the house with the chosen plan and the stones already cut. Several artists would work on one mosaic.
- Tearing paper into small squares and strips.
- Gluing the pieces down with gaps between them to give the appearance of a mosaic.
- Sketching ideas for a design - based on the sun in this case - before deciding which ones to use.

Doing

- With your design in front of you tear pieces of red and yellow paper into small pieces to match your design and arrange them on a square of black sugar paper.
- It may be easier to make the sun shape first

and then fill in the area around it.
- Stick the pieces down carefully as you tear them so that they don't become muddled or lost.
- Leave a small gap between each piece so that it looks like a mosaic.
- Further mosaics could be produced using the computer. (see Step by Step Art Six page 42)

Display

Back the display board in black paper. As all the work is the same shape and the same colour, arrange the pieces as a block, each piece touching its neighbour, in the middle of the board. Add a narrow border of red around the outer edge of the board.

Notable Numbers

Equipment Needed

A computer graphics programme with a grid tool, a line tool, and a fill tool (the programme Dazzle has been used here). A printed sheet showing examples of Roman numerals.

Talk About

* How the Roman Number system was different from ours - it used seven alphabetical signs - **I, V, X, L, C, D** and **M**. Numbers were formed by adding e.g. **6 = V + I = VI** or subtracting e.g. **4 = V - I = IV**. Larger numbers come from Latin words e.g. **C = Centum = 100. M = Mille = 1,000.**

* The shapes of the Roman Numerals and where they are still to be seen e.g. on clocks, at the bottom of pages in some books.

* Drawing lines and shapes around a number that are similar to the shape of the number itself.

* The tools to use on the computer, where they are found on the tool bar and how to get them. How to make the line tool draw thicker and thinner lines by using the right-hand mouse button.

* Using only one colour to fill parts of the finished design.

Doing

* Decide on the Roman numeral you are going to draw - look carefully at its shape and the parts that are thick and the parts that are thin.

* Click on the grid tool with the **left-hand** mouse button. Click on the colour black and then on the line tool with the **left-hand** mouse button. If you want a thick line to start with, click on the line tool with the **right-hand** mouse button and alter its width by dragging the arrow next to it in the box that appears, upwards. Click on **close** and begin drawing the thick parts of your number. To make the line thinner follow the same sequence but drag the arrow next to the line in the box, downwards before clicking on **close** and continuing to draw.

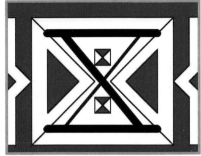

* Once your number is drawn, (still using the colour black, the grid and a thin line) draw a pattern of lines and shapes around the number that are similar to the shape of the number itself.

* Click on the grid tool to remove from the screen with the **left-hand** mouse button, then with the same button click on the fill tool and the colour you want to use. Finally click on those parts of your pattern that you want to fill with colour to complete your design.

Display

Mount the work individually on black and then red and use it as a border around a board on which there is written work about the Romans.

Powerful Portraits

Equipment Needed

Coloured portraits of Tudor noblemen, Henry VIII and Tudor ladies as stimulus material. Photocopies of these to cut up and use as starting points. A range of collage materials in rich colours e.g. felt, vivelle, tissue paper, beads, sequins, foil, feathers etc. Glue, scissors, drawing pencils and black paper and white paper approx A4 size.

Talk About

- The fact that most well known paintings from Tudor times were portraits commissioned by the rich and powerful. The nobility ordered portraits to show their power. They were painted in rich dark colours with serious expressions, in family groups or alone.
- One of the most famous portrait painters of Tudor times was Hans Holbein the younger (1497-1543).
- Finding out more about Hans Holbein and the portraits he painted using the Internet.
- The colours, style and decoration on the Tudor costumes in the portraits. What was worn on the head, hung around the neck etc.
- Choosing from the collage materials rather than using them all.
- Cutting and folding the materials to get different effects.
- Sticking the materials down - how much glue to use and where to put them.

Doing

- Choose one of the photocopied portraits and carefully cut the face out from it.
- Get a piece of A4 paper (either black or white) and place the face on it. Before you glue it down make sure you have left enough space at the top for a hat or head-dress to be added and plenty of room below it for the costume itself.

- Look back at the costume that remains on the photocopy. You now need to add this to your cut out head using a range of collage materials.
- You may want to sketch the shape of the costume in faintly before you begin your collage.
- Your finished portrait should fill most of the paper.
- An alternative approach to this work would be for the children to use a photograph of their own face and add a Tudor costume to it.

Display

Mount the pieces of work individually on a surround of gold foil as if in an ornate frame. Back the display board in red and arrange the portraits in rows with equal spaces between them. If possible include a row of the original portraits in the display.

Making Miniature Portraits

Equipment Needed
Gold card, small pieces of white paper cut into ovals, pencil crayons or felt tip pens, drawing pencils, scissors, glue and collage material. As an alternative to card, clay tiles could be made, cut into ovals, impressed and painted.

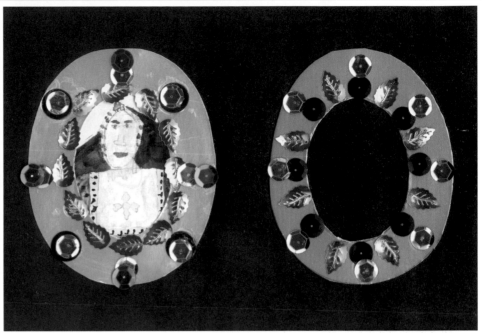

Talk About
- What a miniature is - tiny portraits that became particularly popular during Tudor times. Nicholas Hilliard (1547-1619) the son of a goldsmith became chief portrait painter to Queen Elizabeth I in 1584. He painted beautiful miniatures as well. He first drew his pictures lightly and then built up the details with layers of paint and gold leaf using clear, brilliant colours. His miniatures looked like jewels and were often worn as such.
- Finding out more about miniatures and Nicholas Hilliard on the Internet.
- Drawing a small scale portrait on a small piece of paper - or drawing on larger paper and then reducing it in size using a grid (see Step by Step Art Book 4 page 6) or by using a photocopier. Colouring in the portrait **only** when it is the right size.
- Cutting card into an oval shape and adding decoration using collage material.
- Alternatively cutting a clay tile into an oval shape and adding decoration by impressing.

Doing
- Get a small piece of oval shaped white paper and on it **lightly** sketch a Tudor style portrait. Look carefully at the Tudor portraits for ideas. Now colour it in using pencil crayons or felt tip pens. Look at the Tudor portraits again for ideas.
- Put your oval shaped piece of paper on a piece of gold card and draw round it. Cut the drawn oval out. Fit your portrait on the back of the piece of card so that it shows through the oval cut out shape like a picture in a frame. Cut the outer edge of the card into an oval shape to complete the frame. If clay was being used it would need to be rolled flat and cut in a similar way.
- Decorate the frame of your miniature with collage material. If clay was being used it would need to be impressed with reclaimed materials to add a pattern, and then painted gold. Clay miniatures would need to be glued onto card before being displayed on a wall.

Display
Arrange the miniatures in rows across the board. Add strips of gold paper or yarn to each one to make them appear on chains as if they were being worn. In the centre of the board include the information found on the Internet.

49

Lavish Lace

Equipment Needed
White oil pastels or white wax crayons, white doilies, glue, scissors and pieces of black sugar paper approx 21x 21cm. Pieces of lace and pictures of Tudor ladies and gentlemen wearing ruffs or with lace trimming on their clothes.

Talk About
- Tudor clothes, the Tudor poor wore rough woollen clothes whilst the rich wore clothes made of velvets and satins from Italy and lace from France. Starch which came from Holland meant they could make the stiff collars (Ruffs) that were very popular in Elizabeth's time.
- Finding 'Ruffs' and lace trimmings on the clothes in the pictures.
- Looking at the pieces of lace and describing the patterns on them.
- Finding lines and shapes and how they join and repeat to form a pattern.
- Clothes today that have lace on them.
- Looking for lines, shapes and patterns on doilies and how they repeat and join to form a lace-like pattern.
- The fact that most lace today is made by machine rather than by hand
- Drawing lines and shapes using wax crayon or oil pastel.
- Cutting shapes out of doilies **but** not destroying the doilies completely.

Doing
- Get a piece of black paper and a white doily.
- Decide which parts of the doily you are going to use in your lace pattern and cut them out carefully.
- Arrange them on your piece of black paper - try putting them in the corners or the centre or both.
- When you are happy with your arrangement, stick it down carefully.
- Use a white wax crayon or oil pastel to draw thin lines to join up the different shapes as they would be joined in a piece of lace.
- Draw or add other cut out shapes if you need them to complete your pattern.

Display
Put a picture of a Tudor lady or gentleman wearing a ruff in the middle of the board. Put the title 'Tudor Lace' above or below the picture. Arrange the pieces of work mounted on grey closely together as a border around the picture. Add a black border around the edge of the board and on it arrange the samples of lace looked at before the work was started.

Patterns From Tudor Buildings

Equipment Needed

Pieces of white paper A4 size, strips of black sugar paper in a variety of widths each 21cm long. Glue, scissors, drawing pencils and pictures of black and white Tudor buildings that have a range of different patterns on them.

Talk About

- The great improvements that were made to houses during Tudor times. Many well off people had half timbered houses with stone and brick as a base to stop the damp and a wooden frame on top. These were made of interwoven twigs called wattle. The gaps between were filled with daub, which could be made with mud, chopped straw and manure. Plaster was put over the daub and decorated with timber. Brick chimneys were also added.
- Tudor style modern homes that may be in the locality or a Tudor house that they have visited and what they looked like.
- The different patterns made by the arrangement of the timber on the houses in the pictures. Patterns that are similar and those that are different.
- Folding a strip of paper in half lengthwise and then in half again.
- Cutting shapes out of the top and the bottom of the strip.
- Cutting shapes out of the folds at the edges of the strip but remembering to leave a hinge so that the strip stays intact. Opening the strip to reveal a repeating pattern.

Doing

- Get several strips of black paper of different widths. Fold each one in half **twice**.
- Look at the patterns on the black and white buildings in the pictures and use these for ideas to cut a different type of pattern out of each strip in turn.
- Draw the shapes to be cut out with a pencil first if you want. Remember to leave a hinge at the end of each strip to keep it intact.
- Get a piece of A4 white paper, put it portrait way up and lay the strips across it under each other. Leave gaps between each of the strips.
- When you are happy with your arrangement, stick it down.
- Similar black and white patterns could be drawn on the computer (see Step by Step Art 6 page 58).

Display

Back the board in grey paper with a narrow black border. Put the pictures of Tudor houses that were originally looked at, as a block in the middle of the board. Arrange the rest of the work (unmounted) as a border around them.

Grinning Gargoyles

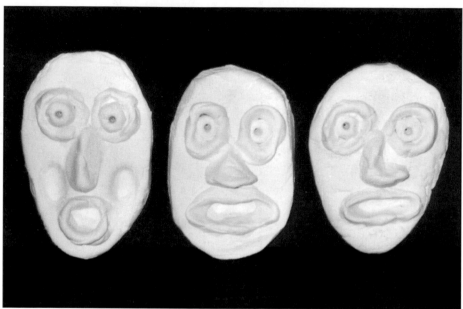

Equipment Needed

Clay, rolling pins, paper towels, cloths or clay boards to put the clay on whilst working to prevent it sticking to the work surface. Reclaimed materials e.g. spatulas, lids etc. to impress into the clay to make shapes and plastic knives to cut the tiles into face shapes. Pictures of gargoyles positioned on buildings.

Talk About

- What they think a gargoyle is and where they are likely to be found.
- How the Tudors decorated the outside of important buildings and churches around the doors, windows, chimneys and buttresses (stone or brick pillars), with carved animals, angels and gargoyles (stone spouts to carry water off a roof, often carved to look like monsters).
- Finding and describing the gargoyles in the pictures.
- Making ugly faces at one other. Which features can and need to be distorted.
- Rolling a ball of clay flat with a rolling pin.
- Prodding and pulling shapes in and on the clay but not joining bits on as these will tend to fall off as the clay dries.
- Impressing reclaimed materials into the clay.

Doing

- Get a piece of clay; put it on a clay board or paper towel before rolling it flat with a rolling pin. It will need to become a fairly thick tile so that features can be pressed and pulled without it collapsing or becoming full of holes.
- Cut the flattened clay into a face shape using a plastic knife.
- You are now ready to add the features -

remember they must be ugly.
- Press and pull eye sockets and bulging eyes.
- Pull a long or short nose. Make it either fat or thin and possibly crooked or turned up. Stroke slight hollows in the clay for the cheeks.
- Press and pull a large socket for the mouth - it could turn up or down or be wide open. Pinch a rim of lips to protrude around the mouth.
- Add final details e.g. pupils to the eyes. Smooth and refine any of the features using the reclaimed materials before allowing the clay to dry.

Display

When the tiles are dry, stick them individually on pieces of black card. Back the board with grey paper. Cut the silhouette of a church out of black paper to go in the middle of the board. On this silhouette display the pictures of gargoyles that the children discussed. Attach the clay tiles on their pieces of card around the edge of the board.

Royal Roses

Equipment Needed

Pipe cleaners or plasticene rolled into thin strips or 'waxworks' (available from Yorkshire Purchasing) and squares of white card 16 x16 cm approx. Alternatively, you could use a computer graphics package with a line tool, a circle tool and symmetry tool (Dazzle was used here). Pictures of the design of the Tudor Rose.

Talk About

- The origins of the Tudor Rose. The Tudor Rose was designed for Henry VII when he married Elizabeth of York. This marriage ended the wars between the Lancastrians and Yorkists. His rose united the white rose of York with the red rose of Lancaster. This motif was often carved to decorate buildings.
- The shape and design and colour of the Tudor Rose.
- Making a drawing with linear material by rolling, twisting and bending it into different shapes.
- If the computer is being used which tools are needed, what they are called, where they are found on the tool bar and how to get them by clicking on them with the left-hand mouse button.

Doing

- Get a piece of white card and the linear material of your choice - it could be one on its own or a combination of several different sorts.

- First bend the material into the shape for the middle of your rose and place it on the card before bending more material to make the shape of the petals. It does not have to be exactly the same as the Tudor rose, just similar.
- Finally add a stem and some leaves to complete the design.
- If the computer is being used - work by clicking the left-hand mouse button each time - first on the symmetry tool, and then the circle tool. Click, hold and drag two circles (one at a time) from the centre where the lines of symmetry cross. Make the inner circle smaller than the outer one.
- Keep the symmetry tool on, click on the line tool, return to the screen and click and drag lines to draw petal shapes around both the large and the small circle. Use the line tool to add some leaf shapes as well.

- Use the fill tool and select colours to fill the shapes you have drawn.

Display

The roses made from linear material will need to be displayed on a flat surface covered with red paper. The computer work, mounted on red could be used as the border round a board of written work about the Tudors.

The Victorians

Fashionable Faces

Equipment Needed

Small paper plates, pipe cleaners, coloured paper, black paper, scissors and glue, paint, cotton wool buds, paintbrushes and pieces of card as mixing palettes. Pictures, books and photographs of Victorian ladies and gentlemen in a range of Victorian costume.

Talk About

- The type of clothes worn by the people in the books and pictures and the way in which the clothes are different from those worn today.
- Who are the wealthy people in the pictures and who are less wealthy - how can you tell?
- In the 1850's the cage crinoline for women made its appearance. These were made from light steel hoops sewn into a special petticoat to make skirts puff out. This was followed by the bustle in the 1870's - a small horsehair pad attached to the waistband at the back to create the look of an ample behind!
- Look for crinolines and bustles in the pictures.
- For men the fashion was for long jackets - frockcoats - waistcoats and close fitting trousers. Hats were of importance to complete an outfit, these included bonnets for women and tall (stove pipe) top hats. Look for these in the pictures.
- The sewing machine was invented during Victorian times which enabled poorer women to copy the styles and fashions of the wealthy.

Doing

- Decide whether your portrait is going to be of a man or a woman and look closely at the books and pictures for information about hats, hairstyles, whiskers etc. that you will need to include.
- Get a paper plate, a paintbrush and some paint on a piece of card and paint your plate pink. When it is dry print the eyes using a cotton bud, add noses and mouths using cut down pipe cleaners. Add a hairstyle and /or whiskers using coloured paper and pipe cleaners that have been bent or twisted.
- Cut out the shape of a top hat or bonnet from coloured paper and add it to the completed plate using masking tape on the reverse sides. Bonnet shapes will need to have their centres cut out so that the face will show through the hole. Add strips of paper as decoration and ribbons to tie under the chin.

Display

Arrange these unmounted faces as a border around the edge of a board on which there is a display of written work about the Victorians.

The Victorians

Simple Samplers

Equipment Needed

A computer graphics programme with a line tool, a text tool, a grid and a fill tool. The programme Dazzle has been used here. Pictures of cross stitch samplers.

Talk About

- What a sampler is and how they were made. Until 1900 girls had to sew and embroider a sampler. It was usually made of canvas and stitched in wool of different colours. Cross stitch was mainly used and patterns focused on patterns from books, the letters of the alphabet, and popular sayings and proverbs. The girl's name and date of birth were also added.
- Sayings e.g. 'Home Sweet Home', 'Waste not want not', that would be appropriate to copy on to a sampler plus what a cross stitch looks like.
- The tools to use on the computer, where to find them and how to get them.
- How to get different fonts and how to change the size of the font.
- The colours to use both for the letters and the background design.
- Using the line tool to draw crosses and patterns for the corner of the sampler.

Doing

- Choose a pale colour for the background of your sampler and click on it with the left-hand mouse button before clicking with the same button on the screen to flood it with colour.
- Click on a new colour for a row of letters with the left-hand mouse button before clicking on the text tool with the right-hand mouse button.

- Boxes will now appear that give you the opportunity to drag arrows downwards to change the font - the style of the text - and the size of the text. (See Step by Step Art 6 pages 25 and 26.)
- Click on OK when you have the size and shape of letters you want, this will return you to the screen so that you can begin the lettering for your sampler.
- Keep the same style of lettering but change the colours for each line or word.
- Click on the line tool and the grid with the left-hand mouse button. Drawing from dot to dot on the grid will help when adding cross stitches and patterns in the corners of the sampler. Alternatively they could be drawn freehand without the grid. Finally print out the finished design.

Display

Mount the samplers individually on brown or black paper. Add thin strips of gold to each side as a frame. Hang the samplers in rows across the board with equal spaces between them. Attach a piece of string or wool to the corners of each one so that they appear to be hanging on the wall.

Making and Painting Plants

Equipment Needed
Small plant pots with **dry** oasis in them. Pipe cleaners or 'Flexiwire', masking tape, green paper and card in assorted shades. Scissors, paint, paintbrushes and pieces of card as palettes. Pieces of white paper A3 size and a collection of houseplants and books about them.

Talk About
*   Houseplants that were popular in Victorian homes, especially aspidistras, ferns and parlour palms and where to find pictures of them. Many other plants also became popular as travel to other parts of the country and the world became faster and more readily available with the invention of the steam engine, the bicycle, the motor car and the steam ship.
*   Finding out more about these inventions from the Internet.
*   Exotic plants were displayed in conservatories and glass houses - look for examples of these e.g. at Kew Gardens and pictures of the Crystal Palace built for the Great Exhibition in 1851.
*   Looking for examples of Victorian style conservatories popular today and the modern materials they are now made of e.g. PVC.
*   The names of the different types of house plants in the collection and if possible their country of origin. The different sizes, shapes and colours of the leaves and stems of the house plants. Drawing and cutting out similar shapes. Mixing different shades of green using paint.

Doing
*   Choose a house-plant and look at its colour and shape before you start.
*   If you are painting a picture of a plant, sketch it first with a pale shade of paint e.g. grey before filling it in with shades of green that you have mixed. Add details e.g. veins to it.
*   If you are making a model, choose the shades of green paper that you need and cut them into the leaf shapes that closely match those of a plant. They will need to vary in size. Tape the leaves on the undersides to pipe cleaners or wire with masking tape. Push the ends of the wire into the dry oasis in a plant pot and then bend some of them over to make them more plant like.

Display
Back the board with green paper, mount the plant paintings individually on black or grey. Divide the board up with strips of white paper like the windows in a conservatory and add a white finial along the top of the board. Display the paintings between the window strips and arrange the 3D plants both on white covered boxes and a flat surface in front of the display.

Working in the Style of a Victorian Artist

Equipment Needed
Pictures that show examples of Turner's work, grey sugar paper A3 size, scissors, glue, chalk pastels, paper towels and colour magazines - travel brochures are particularly useful for this work.

Talk About
- The pictures painted by Turner. What their titles are, what are they about and how they make you feel e.g. Rain, Steam and Speed.
- How to find out more information about Turner and other Victorian artists e.g Millais, Holman Hunt, Landseer etc.
- Landscapes were no longer viewed just as backgrounds to paintings in Victorian times but were popular in their own right. Turner painted landscapes as they had never been seen before - some called him the 'master of coloured light'. He captured movement and mood and did not include many details. His style influenced other artists particularly the 'Impressionists'.
- Creating a landscape by fitting different cut pictures together along the bottom of the paper and leaving a large area to be the sky above the collage.
- Smudging and blending together colouring made using chalk pastels.

Doing
- Get some coloured magazines and from them cut features from different landscapes. Arrange these so that they join up, as naturally as possible along the bottom of a piece of grey sugar paper.
- When you are pleased with your arrangement, stick it down.
- Look carefully at the colours Turner used for his skies and the way they swirled, merged and blended across the paintings.

- Collect similar chalk pastel colours and use them in the same way to add a 'Turner style' sky above your collage landscape. Start from the top of the paper and work downwards to avoid smudging.

- Cover the collage part of your work with a paper towel to protect it. Give your completed picture an appropriate title.

Display
Spray the pastel parts of the drawings with hair spray to fix them before mounting them individually first on black or grey and then on gold. Display some examples of Turner's work and the information

found on the Internet about him in the middle of the board. Arrange the pastel work in rows around it. Print out the titles for the pictures on the computer and add them underneath each one.

Paisley Patterns

Equipment Needed
Pieces of black sugar paper A4 size, silver foil, cerise foil, white paint and white paper (any colour combination could be used as long as all the work is undertaken in these colours so that it can be successfully combined) pencils, scissors, glue and thin strips of card. Pictures of Paisley patterns and fabrics with Paisley designs on them. A collection of shawls.

Talk About
- The shape that makes up a Paisley pattern, where it is found in the examples in the pictures and the different ways in which it is decorated - around the edge and in the centre etc. Shawls were popular with Victorian ladies and were worn both for warmth and as decoration. Shawls were also draped over furniture to further decorate fussy and overcrowded Victorian rooms.
- Finding information about the origins of the shape. It is said to come from India and is based on a mango fruit. Using the Internet, find out about the Scottish town of Paisley where it was imitated and copied on cloth.
- Dressing up in a shawl - how it was worn - and who uses shawls today e.g. mainly babies, old people.
- Drawing the mango shape large enough to fill an A4 piece of paper. Cutting foil and white paper into multiple shapes of a similar size by folding the paper first. Printing lines and dots with the edge of a piece of card dipped in paint.

Doing
- Get a piece of black sugar paper and on it draw a Paisley shape, first with a finger to get an idea of the size it will need to be to fill the paper, and then with a pencil. Cut the shape out carefully.
- Decide where you are going to put the pattern on your shape before choosing the foils and white paper you are going to use. Fold the paper and foil several times before you cut out shapes in order to produce several of them to use in your pattern. Arrange them on your shape and when you are happy with the arrangement, stick them down carefully. Add further detail to your pattern by printing on or between the shapes with the edge of a piece of card dipped in white paint.

Display
Back the board with grey or cerise paper. Drape a piece of black fabric either from the centre or from one side - like a shawl.
Pin the finished Paisley patterns to the fabric with straight pins to add pattern all over it. Include the information found on the Internet at one side or along the bottom of the board.

Striking Silhouettes

Equipment Needed

Pieces of black sugar paper small enough to fit in the centre of a doily, scrap pieces of white paper of the same size to practise on, pencils, scissors, glue, black doilies with a border pattern or white doilies with a border pattern, black paint, paintbrushes and pieces of card both to stick on the doilies and to put the paint on as palettes. Pictures that show heads in silhouette.

Talk About

*   What a silhouette is and what profile means. Where silhouettes are seen today - the present Queen's head appears in profile on stamps, book illustrations are sometimes in silhouette.
*   The Penny post began in 1840. Queen Victoria's head is shown in profile on stamps of the time. Cameo silhouettes cut from black paper were popular with the Victorians. Such pictures were often displayed in frames in Victorian homes.
*   Drawing the profile of a head on a small piece of paper.
*   Cutting the centre out of a black doily **or** painting a white doily black carefully, and allowing it to dry before cutting the centre out of it.

Doing

*   Look carefully at the pictures of the heads in silhouette and at a friend's head in profile. Which bits stick out and protrude and which bits curve in?
*   On scrap pieces of white paper experiment with drawing in pencil different heads in profile. When you are happy with a drawing, copy it on to a piece of black sugar paper and then cut it out carefully.
*   Either cut the centre out of a black doily and stick it on to a piece of card **or** carefully paint a white doily black - remember it will be quite

fragile when wet! - allow it to dry and then cut the centre out of it and stick it on a piece of card.
*   Arrange your cut out silhouette of a head in the cut out centre of the doily to give it the appearance of being in a frame and stick it down.

Display

Back the display board with grey paper. Cut pieces of red crepe paper into long strips. Arrange the strips at intervals with spaces between them from the top to the bottom along the board as though they are ribbons. Cut a 'V' at the bottom of each strip and tie bows in further strips of red crepe paper to go at the top of each strip. Arrange the silhouette pictures on and down each of the red strips with equal spaces between them as if they were on display in a Victorian parlour.

Searchlight Patterns on Fabric

Equipment Needed

Squares of white fabric 16 x 16 cm approx, masking tape, scissors and fabric crayons - (Dylon dye sticks have been used here). Pictures that show the beams of searchlights lighting up the sky plus some torches.

Talk About

*   That during World War Two for nearly a year between Summer 1940 and Spring 1941, the British were subjected to a sustained aerial assault. Air raid sirens would warn of the raids in order that people could take shelter. Air raid wardens patrolled the streets to make sure people took cover, that houselights were not visible and to help with casualties resulting from a raid. At night searchlights sent beams to crisscross the sky to pick out enemy aircraft so that they could be seen more easily and shot down.
*   The path of light that shines from a torch switched on in the dark.
*   Making patterns upwards towards the ceiling using a torch.
*   The colour of the sky when it is lit up by street light, a bonfire or a sunset.
*   Sticking strips of masking tape on to fabric.
*   Crayoning on fabric with fabric crayons.

Doing

*   Get a square of white fabric and some masking tape. Lay the fabric on a flat surface and cut some strips of masking tape to make a crisscross pattern on the fabric.
*   Stick the masking tape on to the fabric remembering to leave plenty of space between each strip. Start sticking the strips along the bottom edge of the square crossing over each another on their way to the top.
*   Get a box of fabric crayons and from it choose the colours discussed for a night sky that is lit up.

*   Colour the fabric by pressing down firmly to fill all the gaps. You can colour on the masking tape as well to make it easier.
*   When you feel your fabric has plenty of strong colour on it, peel off the strips of masking tape to reveal your searchlight pattern.
*   You may want to add small black silhouettes of buildings along the bottom of the fabric.

Display

The searchlight patterns could be mounted on white card and displayed together in the middle of a board backed with black paper or they could be individually

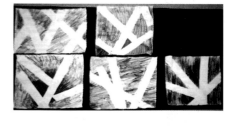

mounted on black card and then red paper and displayed in equally spaced rows around written work about the Blitz.

Remaining Ruins

Equipment Needed

Squares of grey sugar paper 30 x 30 cm approx, chalk pastels, glue and pieces of black paper. Pictures of ruins.

Talk About

- Air raids left many ruined buildings as well as casualties in their wake. London, Birmingham, Bristol, Glasgow, Coventry, Manchester and Liverpool were among the key targets during the war. Raids were often made on the same areas for several nights running, bringing infernos of flames, smashed brickwork, splintered glass and smoke. In the chaos entire streets simply vanished, burying mothers, fathers and children in the rubble.
- Where these cities are and why they were singled out.
- What a ruined building looks like and the shapes of the wall, windows etc. of the ruins in the pictures.
- The colours of the sky lit up at night by a bonfire, a sunset or street lights.
- Tearing large and small shapes out of black paper. Tearing shapes with holes in them out of black paper.
- Colouring with chalk pastel, blending colours together as well as keeping them in their original state.

Doing

- Get a piece of grey sugar paper and some chalk pastel crayons.
- Select the colours previously discussed to represent a night sky that is lit up.
- Working from the top of you paper downwards, add deep patches of colour to different parts of the paper by pressing down firmly with the pastels.
- Keep some of the colours in their original state and merge and blend others together as the patches of colour meet up. Fill all of the paper.

- Get some black paper and tear some shapes that are similar to the shapes of the ruined buildings in the picture. Make sure you have an interesting mixture of shapes of different sizes. Don't try and tear a complete building just bits and pieces.
- Arrange these pieces on your chalk background. When you are happy with your arrangement stick it down carefully trying not to smudge or get chalk on the black paper.

Display

Mount the pieces of work individually on black paper. Back the board in grey paper and arrange the work in equally spaced rows across it. If the gap between each piece of work is narrow the whole display will have greater impact. Alternatively the work could form the border around poetry or creative writing.

Making Hats to Celebrate V E Day

Equipment Needed

Strips of white card 6 cm wide approx, paper plates, scissors, glue, staplers, wax crayons and a range of different types of paper e.g. tissue, cellophane, foil, crepe etc. in red, white and blue. Pictures of the Union Jack flag or actual flags and a collection of paper party hats.

Talk About

- On May 7th 1945 Germany acknowledged defeat. Winston Churchill the Prime Minister and the U S President Harry S.Truman agreed that the following day, May 8th should be celebrated as Victory in Europe (V E) Day. Crowds streamed into the streets and that night street lights were switched on all over Britain for the first time since the outbreak of war. London's rejoicing crowds flocked around Buckingham Palace and throughout the country there was dancing and singing in the street.
- Occasions which we celebrate now and how we celebrate them.
- The styles of the party hats and the ways in which they are decorated.
- The pattern on the Union Jack flag.
- How to use a stapler to fasten pieces of card together.
- Pressing on firmly when colouring with wax crayons to achieve dense colour.
- Fringing, curling, twisting and cutting paper into different shapes.

Doing

- Get three strips of white card and a stapler. Fasten the ends of one strip together to make a headband. Fasten another strip to make an arch from the front to the back of the band. Fasten the third strip to make an arc that overlaps the first and

goes from the left to the right of the band.

- You now need to decorate this framework using the different, red, white and blue papers.

- Once the frame work is covered you may want to decorate it further by drawing and adding flags or paper flowers to it or adding a paper plate to the top or side of the framework. Add curls, fringes, flags etc. to that.
- Experiment with different ideas before you glue them down to make a stunning piece of headwear.

Display

Arrange the hats on a flat surface covered in red or blue paper. Back the board behind it in the same colour. Decorate the edge of the board with flags that have red,

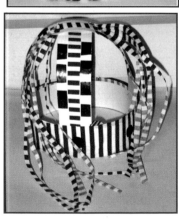

white and blue patterns drawn on them with wax crayons and the cut out silhouettes of hands (drawn on black paper). Arrange photographs of the children making and wearing their hats on a contrasting block of either red or blue paper in the middle of the board.

Pop Culture - Work in the Style of Andy Warhol

Equipment Needed

A computer graphics package with drawing tools, a fill tool, a square shape and select area and tile facility (Dazzle has been used here). Drawing pencils, squares of white paper 10 cm x 10cm approx, oil pastel crayons and examples of Andy Warhol's work particularly his prints that show several versions of the same image in different colours.

Talk About

*   What pop art is and when it became popular. From the late 1950's and throughout the 1960's there was unprecedented interest in popular (pop) music, films, magazines and the world of fashion and advertising. Several artists borrowed some of these techniques and motifs for their work. This new form of art became known as Pop Art.
*   Finding out more about Pop Art and Pop Artists including examples of their work using the Internet.
*   The bright, psychedelic colours used in Pop Art and how they could be described.
*   How artists produced identical images of the same object filled with different colours - by screen printing.
*   How we could produce several identical images using either a photocopier or a computer.

Doing

*   On the computer, click on a brush with the left-hand mouse button and draw, in black, a simple image on the screen.
*   Click on the square shape with the left-hand mouse button and draw a square around the image. Now click on the select area tool with the left-hand mouse button and draw a box round this square.
*   Go to Area on the top tool bar and click the left-hand mouse button. Go down to the word 'Tile', click again and your shape will fill the screen as a repeat pattern.

*   Use the fill tool and bright colours similar to those of Andy Warhol to fill each image. Use the same colours for each image but combine them in different ways. (See Step by Step Art 6 page 40.)
*   Draw a simple image in pencil on a square piece of paper. Photocopy this image several times using the photocopier. Colour each image in using oil pastels using bright colours similar to those of Andy Warhol. Use the same colours for each image but combine them in different ways. Stick the images together as a block on a larger piece of paper.

Display

Back the board in blue. Mount the blocks of work on black and display them as a group in the middle of the board. Mount the computer work on black and cerise and use it as a border around the edge of the board. Alternatively, use the computer work on its own as a border around relevant written work.

Terrific Trainers

Equipment Needed

Drawing pencils, (4b-6b), pieces of white paper A4 size, paint, paintbrushes and pieces of card for use as mixing palettes. A collection of trainers of different sizes and with different designs on them.

Talk About

- The popularity of jogging as a way of keeping fit that became a focus for many people in recent decades. Alongside this, marathon runs have been staged annually in different parts of the world. Fashion has used and followed this 'keep fit' trend by producing trainers in constantly changing styles and with that all important 'designer logo' on them.
- The trainers on display, those that the children themselves own, those they like most - and least and why - and the logos that they are familiar with.
- The cities in which marathon runs take place and more information about them from the Internet.
- Drawing lines, tones and textures using a pencil to get different effects.
- Looking at trainers from different viewpoints and not just the front.

Doing

- Put a trainer on the surface in front of you and carefully turn it around until you have the view you want to draw.
- Draw the shape of the trainer on the paper with a finger to get an idea of the size it will need to be to fill the paper.
- Get either a pencil or a paintbrush and a pale shade of paint e.g. grey. On the paper draw the outline shape of the shoe. Next, add further outlines of the shapes and patterns that decorate it.

- Fill in these shapes and add any further textures and patterns by using different lines and dots. Fill in any dark areas that you see e.g. the opening to the inside by pressing down firmly with a pencil to create different tones. If it is a painting you can achieve the same effect by using different shades of paint i.e. by making colours lighter and darker.
- If your work is a painting fill in the surrounding area with shapes in the colours that match those of your trainer.

Display

Mount the pencil sketches individually on black paper and display them in rows with equal spaces between them on a board backed in red. Mount the paintings also on black and display them in similar equally spaced rows but back the board in grey or blue. Display the actual trainers on a flat surface beneath the display.